WHICH WAY
IS CAMP?

WHICH WAY IS CAMP?

AN ETHIOPIAN, SPIRITUAL ADVENTURE

DAVID E. BRECKENRIDGE

TWO HARBORS PRESS

Minneapolis

TWOHARBORS
WWW.TWOHARBORSPRESS.COM

Two Harbors Press
212 3rd Avenue North, Suite 290
Minneapolis, MN 55401
612.455.2293
www.TwoHarborsPress.com

ISBN-13: 978-1-62652-061-5
LCCN: 2013903894

Distributed by Itasca Books

Printed in the United States of America

DEDICATION

This book is dedicated to my wife,
Marcia R. Flugsrud-Breckenridge, MD, PhD.
Without her continued loving support and encouragement
this book could not have been written.

ACKNOWLEDGMENTS

I want to thank all of my friends, family, and others who have given me encouragement and many helpful suggestions:

Dr. Don McClure and his wife, Lyda; the three other "boys" who helped make it happen: Dave, Chuck, and Charlie; the Anuak people of the village at the Gilo River who worked with us and were our gracious and hospitable neighbors; my Nuer blood brother, Gatqwath; and the West Allis, Wisconsin, United Presbyterian Church, which provided travel expenses for this adventure.

Special thanks to Betty (Bott) Calderwood, my Sterling College classmate, who, through e-mails and phone call "nudges," kept asking me, "How is the book coming along?"

Lastly, I want to give special thanks to my editor, Rachel Fichter, for her thorough editing and excellent suggestions for improving the manuscript. However, any errors in this book are my responsibility.

TABLE of CONTENTS

MESSAGE TO DAVE
A Taste of What Follows

"*Message to Dave! Message to Dave!*" When I realized the small airplane circling high overhead would not, could not, land at our camp, I ran quickly to my tent to grab the small portable radio and tuned frantically for the frequency for aircraft transmissions. Those cryptic words were the first thing I heard when I picked up the thin mechanical sound of the airplane's radio. **"Message to Dave, Message to Dave, do not hunt, do not fish, do not leave camp. A message will follow in a few days!"** These words were repeated several times. Then I saw the airplane turn toward the west and disappear in the direction of Sudan. My heart sank! This was the airplane that was to have reconnected us to civilization. Instead, as I watched in dismay, the airplane, whose droning engine had briefly lifted our spirits, flew out of sight. Our only connection to civilization had disappeared. Four young American men stranded in the African wilderness of western Ethiopia, isolated from all but native people whose language we did not understand, nor did they understand ours. It was sixty miles from the closest settlement that was not a native African hut—sixty

Map of Eritrea & Ethiopia.

CHAPTER ONE

1960:
A DOOR CLOSES,
ANOTHER DOOR OPENS

In January of 1960[1] I was halfway through my first year of semi-nary. My wife of a year and a half and I were returning from a rare meal out at a very nice restaurant with a number of my fellow seminarians and their wives. As we climbed the stairs to our second-floor apartment, she suddenly gave a sharp cry and collapsed on the stairs. She was immediately unconscious. One of the students with us called for an ambulance. It seemed to take hours before the ambulance arrived, but only a few minutes later we were on the way to the hospital, one of the longest rides of my life. It was shortly after we arrived at the emergency room of Presbyterian Hospital that the doctor came out to talk with me. He said that my wife had a massive brain hemorrhage from a ruptured aneurism and it did not look good. It wasn't. Shortly after that she died without regaining consciousness.

---

1. Note to the reader: this is written fifty years after the events. Any errors in fact are due to inaccuracies of my memory. I lost all my notes and pictures in the Katrina flood.

The shock of her death made it a difficult struggle for me to finish that spring semester. The loving care and support of the faculty and seminary students made it possible for me to continue. Toward the end of the semester, a friend asked me what my plans were for the summer. I told him I had no idea what I would do. He knew that I was having a lot of difficulty just getting through week to week. He suggested that I consider going as a summer student pastor to his home church in West Allis, Wisconsin. He encouraged me to talk with the pastor of the West Allis church, Bryon Crozier, who would be near Pittsburgh in a couple of weeks. At that time in my life, having someone suggest a plan for me was a huge relief. I met with Bryon, his wife, Beth, and their two young boys. We had a good visit and Bryon offered me the position, which I readily accepted. That summer in West Allis, working with the young people of the church was a wonderful break. I was able to get some distance from my grief and enjoy my involvement with full-of-life young people. I had lots of fun with them and they seemed to enjoy my participation.

Around the middle of the summer, the church people, young and older alike, began buzzing with excitement. When I caught on that something special was going to happen, I asked what it was. They said, "Don McClure is coming to preach at the morning service and then give a talk at the dinner we're having for him." When I asked who Don McClure was, they were stunned. Everyone knew about him, except me. I had not been raised in the United Presbyterian Church and had only begun to

gain some knowledge of it in the past three years. I had not had
the opportunity to hear of Dr. Don McClure.

Though I was studying to be a Presbyterian pastor, I had not been raised Presbyterian. In the small town of
Woodston, Kansas, where I grew up, there was a Pentecostal
church, a Methodist church, and our church, the United Brethren. We "belonged" to the United Brethren, which became,
after mergers, the United Methodist Church of today. Quite
a few people in the smaller denominations felt that they were
losing some of their religious purity by merging with a more
liberal, larger church. Change, especially religious change, does
not come easily on these Western prairies.

After being discharged from the US Army, I chose to
go to Sterling College in Sterling, Kansas, a conservative Christian college. At that time it was sponsored by the United Presbyterian Church. This small college fit well with my religious
"adolescence" at the time. My rather restricted view of Christian faith would soon be challenged as I was exposed to a much
richer view of spirituality. While attending Sterling I became
impressed with the United Presbyterian Church and especially
their form of church government. I felt I was called to be a
minister and wanted, specifically, to be a Presbyterian minister.
I then attended Pittsburgh Theological Seminary, where I was
immediately exposed to a much wider view of Christian faith.

The Presbyterian branch of Protestantism in America
has the same history of splintering as most of the other major
denominations. In 1958, one year before I began seminary

his return to Ethiopia. Dr. McClure told us His Majesty, Haile Selassie, had personally invited him to open a new mission station on the Gilo River. It would be sixty miles beyond any other developed settlement. It would bring a medical clinic, a school, and also the mission church far into that undeveloped region. An unspoken part of the emperor's desire to have a mission in this remote region was to provide an outpost to help protect the border with Sudan from incursions. The conflict between the two nations had already begun to heat up. I do not believe Dr. McClure knew of this secondary purpose.

Dr. McClure told us that as part of that new project he would be inviting a group of young men to join him as volunteers for a year. They would help build the new mission station on the Gilo River. After the evening meeting, I had an opportunity to visit with Don and asked him more about the volunteer program. He told me more about it and said that he still had a few slots open but would have to complete his selections by October in order to prepare for his return to Ethiopia in September of the following year.

In September, I wrote to Don McClure to tell him I would like to join his volunteer group. I heard nothing for three weeks and had begun to get quite discouraged. When I got Don's letter, he was very apologetic. My letter kept bouncing around trying to catch up with him, as he had moved his temporary residence several times. He told me he would be delighted to have me and was counting on my "life experience" to be of real value to him and the project. Neither he nor I knew how prophetic that statement would be. Now I had something to look forward to other than classes. This exciting prospect enabled me to successfully complete the next year. The West Allis United Presbyterian Church generously offered to pay for my travel expenses to Ethiopia.

It turned out that the four of us going as volunteers were living in the Pittsburgh, Pennsylvania, area. Chuck and Charlie were University of Pittsburgh students from the Mt. Lebanon United Presbyterian Church. The other Dave and I were both students at Pittsburgh Theological Seminary. This made it easy for us to get together from time to time during the year and for Don to meet with us a couple of times to help us prepare for our trip and our year in Ethiopia.

Don was very helpful in advising us about preparations. He and the mission would help arrange for travel documents. We would need to get our own passports, visas, and shots. Don was quite specific in what we should and could not take. He told us we had to minimize what we brought with us as space would be very tight when we began the overland trip by Land Rover. We were to pack only one suitcase or duffel bag. I chose my army duffel bag. It turned out to be an ideal choice. You could really stuff things into it and it was almost indestructible.

Don advised a good, sturdy camera that did not require any batteries and as much film as we could afford. (No digital cameras then.) He suggested we bring some books to read and a couple of flashlights. He would supply batteries for us. We were also told to bring one pair of tennis shoes that we could expect to wear out and toss. It turned out that our Anuak friends loved every item we left, even if we thought it was of no more use. If we required any prescription medication, we would need to bring a year's supply, as well as writing supplies to last a year. He said we would need one dress outfit with shirt and tie as there would likely be a few occasions when we would need to "dress up." I found a gabardine suit that was perfect; I could roll it up and stuff it in my duffel bag, and when I shook it and let it hang overnight, it looked just fine. The shoes I wore with that outfit would be what I wore on my return to the States. We would need a light jacket (even near the equator, at 8,000 feet it's chilly). He suggested two pairs of jeans and three pairs of shorts, one pair to hold in reserve as casual dress if needed.

Don would supply sunscreen and insect repellent. I talked with several people who had spent some time in quite primitive (by American standards) conditions, and they suggested that I get a copy of *Lange's Medical Handbook*, a thick paperback. That purchase turned out to be of great importance. I needed prescription glasses, so I bought an extra pair and a pair of prescription sunglasses. I had saved the small compact sewing kit I had from the army and brought it with me, another very useful addition. The needles were invaluable for removing thorns and splinters. I brought a small pocket dictionary and an animal and plant guide to Africa. I have always liked maps, but I had a very hard time finding any maps of Ethiopia with much detail.

Finally the day for our departure was near. I had my passport, all my shots, and my visa to go to Ethiopia. The seminary graciously allowed me to pack my things and store them in one of their storage lockers until my return. I would travel by bus to New York and meet up with Dr. McClure and his wife at the hotel where they were staying before departure. I was both excited and apprehensive about my travel to New York, as I had never been to the Big Apple. It would be an all-day bus ride leaving very early and arriving late afternoon. It would also be my first experience traveling through the Appalachian Mountains on the historic Pennsylvania Turnpike. Today we are so used to traveling on the interstate system that it's hard to imagine traveling without it. The Pennsylvania Turnpike was one of the major projects of the WPA during the depression. The turnpike officially opened October 1, 1940, and was built using an old railroad route and some of the old railroad tunnels. In the tunnels the road was just two lanes, one each way. I never quite got used to going through those seven tunnels on a big bus and meeting heavy truck traffic head on.

Fortunately the trip was uneventful and I arrived at Union Station safe and sound. I took a taxi to the hotel where I met the other three fellows and Don and Lyda. We spent a day in New York before boarding the freighter the following morning. The ship was docked toward the upper end of the docks on the Hudson. The ship was scheduled to leave the dock before noon, so we would get to see Lower Manhattan, pass by the Statue of Liberty, and go through the Verrazano Narrows on our way out to sea. Don had been in the city supervising the packing and loading of the extensive amount of goods they a shower barely large enough to turn around in, an upper and lower locker for some clothing, and one chair. All our cabins were on the outside facing the deck, so we did have a small window. Clearly we would not spend any more time than necessary for sleeping in our cabins. We were invited to visit the bridge when the sign stating we were allowed on the bridge was posted. We could use the officers' mess as a lounge until half an hour before mealtime. In the mess there was posted a large map of the Atlantic. The crew charted our progress on the map by placing a stickpin at the location of the ship at each mealtime. The pin location included a small note with the latitude, longitude, time, date, and current speed. On the bulletin board beside the map was posted the weather forecast for the day.

Dinner that evening was special. We had been asked to "dress" for dinner. I was glad that shortly after we had gotten to our cabins I had taken out my gabardine suit, dress shirt, and tie and hung them so the wrinkles would come out. For this dinner, all of the ship's crew, including the mess crew, were wearing dress uniforms. They looked very sharp.

We were served champagne before the meal, and the captain offered a toast to his guests. Don reciprocated and toasted the captain and crew. The captain then gave a short speech welcoming us, told a brief history of the vessel, and introduced us to each one of the crew members. He also told us that a film would be shown in the mess about an hour after the meal was finished. The meal was excellent! We were served an outstanding prime rib. I felt the chef was going to have to work hard to keep up this level of quality. It did not seem to be much of a challenge; all the meals, including breakfast, were outstanding. The only problem was that the meals were so good that on those very few occasions when something was slightly less than perfect, you noticed it.

Midafternoon of the second day, the seas began to pick up and the ship pitched and rolled more strongly with the waves. You had to be careful when you went outside and hold on when you walked. Fortunately, I did not get seasick, but with the rocking and rolling, two of my colleagues became quite sick. They had a couple of miserable days before they began to recover.

The following day we had quite rough seas. I was really enjoying the waves crashing against and over the bow. Not realizing that I was not supposed to be there, I had walked to the bow to experience the full effect. It was very exhilarating. After I had been there a short time, a crew member came to me and asked what I was doing up there. I told him I was enjoying the waves. He told me I could not be up there, so I returned with him. Not long after I left the bow and returned to our cabin, we were told to don our life jackets and to keep them on at all times, even when sleeping! Later I learned that we were in the outer edges of Hurricane Betsy, which had stalled right in our path. The captain spent three days trying to avoid the worst of the storm. Due to the heavy seas, the ship could only maintain a very slow speed. Our trip to Cadiz, Spain, had been estimated to take five days, but it took us eight days! I also realized that the captain was very concerned about the effect the heavy seas could have on those locomotives on deck. If one of them had broken loose, it would have been a disaster. We were in good hands.

The day before our arrival in Cadiz, we were told that we would probably arrive outside the port in the middle of the night and the ship would drop anchor to wait for morning to come into dock. That night I got up from my bunk several times to look out and see if I could see land. I wanted to glimpse Europe at the first opportunity. Finally, at about 2 a.m., I spotted lights and then more lights, until I could clearly see we were approaching a coastline. I stayed up to watch. As the ship approached the harbor I could see the beacon lights guiding us toward the harbor. The closer we got, I could see that it was a huge harbor. As we drew nearer to the harbor, the ship began to slow. Just inside the mouth of the harbor, the ship came to a full stop and I heard the anchor chains rattle as the anchor dropped. Later when I looked at the map, I saw that Cadiz was really a rather small city sitting on the end of a narrow peninsula that forms the mouth of the harbor. There are three larger cities protected by the harbor. The largest is El Puerto de Santa Maria, smaller is San Fernando, and smaller yet but still much larger than Cadiz is Puerto Real.

I tried to get some sleep but it was very fitful. Just as dawn was breaking I heard the rattle of the anchor chains being hauled in. Shortly after that the ship began to move. We were coming into harbor. Since we had been anchored only a short distance away from Cadiz, all the ship had to do was turn around and head into the dock, a matter of minutes.

We were only in Cadiz a few hours, but I really enjoyed my first taste of Europe. The city was the cleanest I had ever seen. It looked as if you could eat off of the narrow cobblestone streets. There was not a piece of trash anywhere. From Cadiz we went through the narrow Strait of Gibraltar that separates the Atlantic Ocean from the Mediterranean Sea. The strait is only nine miles wide at its narrowest point but nearly 3,000 feet deep and separates Europe from Africa. The impressive Rock of Gibraltar literally stands guard over the passage. The "Rock" remains nominally the property of the United Kingdom, having been transferred to Britain by the Treaty of Utrecht of 1713. Twice the residents of Gibraltar rejected Spain's attempt to claim the Rock and its inhabitants. Gibraltarians are now self-governed under the terms of the constitution of 2006. Due to its strategic location, the Rock became an important Royal Navy base, acting as a key defensive site for Britain during World War II, guarding all shipping through the strait. The British had a total of 30,000 troops from all branches of military services stationed at Gibraltar.

The limestone rock stands 1,398 feet high, so from the top it commands an impressive view of all the surrounding land and sea. It is a very interesting geological formation. It is an overturned fold of limestone strata, so the youngest layers are on the bottom and the oldest on top. The porous nature of the limestone allowed gun fortifications to be dug into it with connecting tunnels. Visiting these "Great Siege Tunnels" is a key tourist attraction today. A total of six tunnels for embrasures were constructed by 1797.

After passing through the strait, our ship sailed along the north coast of Africa close enough that we could see buildings and sometimes vehicles on the roadways. The ship passed through the Strait of Sicily. Seeing how close Sicily is to North Africa at the point of Tunisia, I could understand why Sicily was so important to the Allies in World War II. We passed between Sicily and the Island of Malta over to Greece, where we docked at Piraeus Greece.

During the day spent there, I took the opportunity to climb up to the top of the Acropolis (*acro polis* means high city) and stand in the Parthenon. It's amazing that these ancient structures still exist. The construction of the Parthenon began in 447 BC and continued until 438 BC. It was built as a temple for the Greek Goddess Athena, for whom the city of Athens is named. Athena is the protector of the city and goddess of wisdom, courage, inspiration, civilization, warfare, strength, strategy, female arts, crafts, justice, and skill. With such a list of responsibilities, she certainly deserved such an impressive temple built for her. The Parthenon is 228 feet long, almost a football field in length, and 101 feet wide. Each of the forty-six massive outside columns is six feet in diameter and thirty-four feet tall.

From Greece, we crossed the Mediterranean to Alexandria, Egypt. Each day we encountered another amazing world, culture, language, people, and dress. Places and people I had read about and pictured in my mind were suddenly real, and I was in their midst. I loved every minute of it. History began to come alive for me. As we were leaving the harbor at Piraeus there was a pod of dolphins playing near the mouth of the bay. Then as we continued out to sea and gained speed, four of them followed and surfed in the bow waves, two on each side of the ship. What a great sight that was.

* * *

Google a map of Greece and you will see that the Aegean Sea is dotted with hundreds of small islands. We passed by many small islands on our way toward Crete. I then understood why this part of the Mediterranean was so dangerous to the early sailors; their ships were often blown onto the rocks of these islands in storms. It is also why this region is such a rich research area for marine archeologists.

We crossed the Mediterranean, passing by the island of Crete on our way to Alexandria. I was surprised to see the snow-capped mountain range that ran the length of Crete from west to east. The highest of these mountains is over 8,000 feet. Crete is believed to be the center of Europe's first advanced civilization, the Minoan, which flourished between 2700 and 1420 BC. Crete is also rich in mythology. The god Zeus was supposed to have been born in a cave on Mt. Ida.

We docked at the Port of Alexandria and were there only a few hours while they lifted the large diesel locomotives off the fore deck for their destination in Egypt. While the locomotives were being unloaded, Don had a person from the American mission take us on a brief tour to the mission. One sight that stands out in my mind was the heavily laden date palm trees that seemed to line every street. I could see why dates were so popular in that region.

Alexandria has no natural harbor. When Alexander the Great founded the city, and named it for himself, he created a harbor by having his engineers excavate an existing smaller anchorage that had silted in. He is believed to have built the first breakwaters to protect the harbor. Alexander chose this site for his base of operations in the Eastern Mediterranean, and the city became a great cosmopolitan center in the ancient world. Ptolemy, Alexander's successor, founded a great university called a "museum," or home of the Muses. Several of the great mathematicians of antiquity, such as Euclid, Archimedes, and Eratosthenes, were connected to this learning center. Eratosthenes' calculation for the circumference of the Earth was remarkably accurate given the limitations in measuring that he faced. He calculated the circumference to be 36,690 kilometers, an error of less than 2 percent.

The library at Alexandria became the greatest in the ancient world. Unfortunately the great library was destroyed, possibly accidently when Julius Caesar, in 48 AD, burned his fleet of ships in the harbor and the fire spread to the part of the city where the library was located. Or, it may have been destroyed by the early Christian church, established in Alexandria around 391 AD. Finally, when the Muslim Caliph Omar took over the city in 640 AD, he is reported to have said that whatever was in the library that would contradict the Koran must be destroyed.

We entered the Suez Canal at Port Said. Our ship then took us through the Suez Canal to the Red Sea. The Suez Canal is not very wide. It is not wide enough for two ships to meet and pass safely. So there are a few passing bays where ships can wait for oncoming ships. A canal from the Mediterranean to the Red Sea was actually studied by Napoleon Bonaparte in the late 1700s. He had hoped to cause trade difficulties for the British. Due to a miscalculation, it was not attempted. His engineers miscalculated and thought there was a significant difference in the sea levels of the Red Sea and the Mediterranean. Actually there is very little difference in the sea levels; the Suez is a "sea level" canal. Construction of this earth-banked canal began in 1859 and was opened ten years later in 1869. The canal is 120 miles long, 79 feet deep, and 673 feet wide. Since the banks are earth, ships must go slowly to prevent undue erosion.

Because we were traveling so slowly, it took us a day to pass through the canal. Once as I was standing on deck watching the sights, I noticed we seemed to be getting closer to the bank. There were buoys along each bank to mark how close a ship could safely go without hitting the bank. Suddenly I felt the ship turn sharply as it brushed the buoy near the bank. I guess someone wasn't watching where he was supposed to be watching. Just another close call that passed safely thanks to the One who is watching over us in all ways.

We left the Suez Canal at Port Suez and entered the Red Sea. There are many theories about the reason for the name. Two that make logical sense are: the Red Sea is very salty and has a coral that is red in color, which is only found there; second, there is an algae there that is red in color when it blooms. The Red Sea is part of the Great Rift caused by the African plate separating from the Asian plate. The separation continues today at a rate of about half an inch per year. In geological terms, that's a pretty fast clip. The same rift that formed the Red Sea begins in the Dead Sea in Israel and continues to the Rift Valley that cuts Ethiopia from the Bay of Djibouti in the east to Lake Turkana in Kenya in the southwest. The Red Sea is 1,400 miles long, 220 miles wide at its widest, and 7,254 feet deep at its deepest, with an average depth of 1,600 feet. It is a big sea! The average surface water temperature at the north end is 79 degrees, and 86 degrees at the south, bath water temperature. It only varies about 2 degrees between summer and winter, as the equator is only a few hundred miles south of the southern end of the Red Sea and passes through Kenya south of Ethiopia. The sea is exceptionally clear and full of sea life. At night, as the ship stirred the water, the phosphorescence was spectacular. It provides some of the best scuba diving and snorkeling in the world. Its coral reefs are still quite healthy. Another delightful sight was the schools of flying fish flitting from the waves alongside the ship.

We docked at Port Sudan for a few hours. Actually we didn't dock, we anchored just outside, as the docks there could not accommodate a ship as large as ours. Small boat "taxis" took us from the ship to shore. While the ship was off-loading cargo for Port Sudan, we went to the only hotel in town for lunch. There were no paved streets. The hotel looked like a scene from

Lawrence of Arabia. The hotel was a two-story, white-washed structure with tall open windows all around the lower level with a wide balcony overhanging the lower level. The upper level housed the guest rooms. The windows on the second floor were tall, but not as tall as the lower ones, and all were shuttered. It was near midday in September and, in this desert country, very hot and dry. When we entered the high-ceilinged lobby, I was surprised how much cooler it was inside than outside. Hanging from the ceiling were a number of slow-turning ceiling fans, turning just fast enough to stir the air but not enough to make a breeze. We had a light lunch of cheese and bread with sparkling mineral water. We knew we could make up for this when we returned to the ship.

The most interesting thing about our visit to Port Sudan was actually seeing the "fuzzy wuzzies" made famous by Kipling's poem "Fuzzy-Wuzzy."

> *"So 'ere's to you, Fuzzy-Wuzzy, at your 'ome in the Soudan;*
> *You're a pore benighted 'eathen but a first-class fightin' man."*[2]

The fuzzy wuzzies are so named because of their hair-dos. They may have been the inspiration for the American blacks' Afro. They are the Hadandoa tribe of eastern Sudan, and some scholars believe that the pharaohs descended from these tribes. The men all wore long flowing white cotton robes with loose sleeves (called thobe or thawb). When they were working, the robe was gathered by the lower hem between their legs and tied up at the waist, looking somewhat like jodhpurs. The men

2. Kipling, Rudyard (1865-1936) (Soudan Expeditionary Force)

all carried the traditional Jambiya dagger or knife that is unique to the Islamic world. It has the typical curved, ten-inch double-edge blade, with the I-shaped grip. These knives have designs that identify them as belonging to a particular tribe. The knives look very lethal and I imagine they can be. We were only in Port Sudan a few hours and then took a water taxi back to our ship. It was a great relief to be back in the air-conditioned comfort of the ship. When the ship was moving, it wasn't too bad outside, but with no air, it was rather miserable.

After our brief stop at Port Sudan, we enjoyed two more days of sailing in the beautiful Red Sea. The seagoing part of our adventure was about to end and the land journey was about to begin. Our ship docked at the Port of Massawa, Eritrea. Our first night off ship we stayed in the Belle View Hotel in Massawa while Dr. McClure's supplies were unloaded and then packed onto trucks for shipment to Gambela. Dr. McClure took delivery of two new Land Rovers, a vehicle similar to the U.S. Willys Jeep. These Land Rovers were at least as tough and capable as the Jeep, if not tougher. We were to become very acquainted with just how tough and capable on our thousand-mile journey. Half of that trip would be on roads that were nothing more than trails.

I am quite sure that the Belle View Hotel was the best available in 1961, although it would not have gained a single star in any traveler's guide. We "boys" stayed in one room; Dr. McClure and his wife, Lyda, stayed in another. The rooms had ceiling fans, no air conditioning, beds that had woven rope to support the cotton mat "mattresses," and tall louvered windows leading to a balcony. Oh yes, the bathroom was down the hall, but it boasted an actual sit-down commode, not just a hole in the floor as we had on brief ship stops along the coast of Africa.

We had a room with a "view," so we opened the tall louvered shutters and stepped out onto the very narrow balcony to see what kind of view it was. Imagine our surprise when we looked directly onto other balconies across a narrow alley and the view was pretty amazing, especially to four young men. We were looking onto balconies and sometimes into the rooms of young women in very skimpy attire. It turned out that this was a local house of prostitution. We quickly dubbed our room the "belly view" and decided that was really the correct pronunciation of the Belle View Hotel! The next day began our road trip from Massawa to Asmara, Eritrea.

This is the view and the kind of switchbacks we encountered
on the drive from Massawa to Asmara.

CHAPTER THREE

BELLY VIEW HOTEL:
MASSAWA TO ADDIS ABABA

The drive from Massawa to Asmara was an interesting drive on a paved road that climbed from sea level to 7,300 feet. About five miles from Massawa, we got into hills, and by twenty miles we were seriously climbing. Some of the views from the many switchbacks were awesome. I had some difficulty enjoying the view since none of the other fellows had any experience driving in mountains. When they drove, I was holding onto my seat and trying to hold the Land Rover on the road with the intensity of my staring at the edge of the road. The only time I was relaxed enough to somewhat enjoy the view was when I was driving; even then, all of my attention needed to be on the road. We had left the hot, dry desert only a short time ago, but the climate had changed radically. It was actually cool. There was lush vegetation and we began to drive through clouds. What a change of experience that was. There were few guardrails or barriers of any kind protecting us from a plunge of hundreds,

sometimes thousands, of feet. The road had been built by the
Italians to transport goods and equipment up the escarpment
to the plateau.

When we reached the plateau, we drove through countryside and by many small villages. The road wound through
valleys that were heavily terraced and cultivated, bordered by
still higher mountain ridges. The small villages were a mixture
of thatched-roof houses made of sticks and plastered with mud
and houses that appeared to be made of concrete blocks that
were plastered. Some of these houses also had thatched roofs
and some tile. While these villages were poor, they were far
better than we would see when we reached Ethiopia. Each village had at least one store combined with a gas station. Some
even advertised places to eat. This part of the country received
quite a lot of rainfall and was lush and green. There were many
flowers, even roses blooming around some of the houses in the
villages. Since this was our first experience in this part of the
country, we did not realize what a contrast Eritrea would make
with Ethiopia. Here in Eritrea the many people did not appear
to be terribly poor, destitute, and undernourished as we would
see later in Ethiopia. We also did not see any beggars. The difference in the state of the people and the living conditions in
Eritrea was due to the influence of and aid received from the
Italian occupation and then, after the war, from British administration. While these were by no means unmixed blessings,
clearly the people in Eritrea were in much better condition than
the majority in Ethiopia.

We arrived in the early afternoon at the very nice home of Dr. Glen Reed. Dr. Reed was the United Presbyterian Regional Secretary for Africa. His home was in a very pleasant neighborhood that could have been an older neighborhood in Florida or California. The streets were paved and the lawns were nicely maintained. The landscape, of course, was tropical, the style of home was Mediterranean, and all yards were fenced. This would be the last we would see of this level of "Western" lifestyle, except for a few neighborhoods in Addis Ababa.

* * *

Early the next morning, we began the first leg of our road trip to Addis Ababa. Don, Lyda, and one of us four "boys" would ride in one Land Rover and the other three would ride in the other Land Rover. Both vehicles were packed to the limit and had jerry cans of gasoline and drinking water tied front and rear to both Land Rovers. We filled the water cans at Dr. Reed's house. The seven-hundred-mile road from Asmara to Addis Ababa, the capital of Ethiopia, was a gravel and dirt road. There were no motels or hotels and very few places where we could buy gasoline, and no place for safe drinking water.

About one hundred miles from Asmara, we stopped at the border checkpoint to cross into Ethiopia. Fortunately, Dr. McClure had a personal letter from Emperor Haile Selassie that worked magic with every official we encountered—and there were many, especially police. All of them were expecting to get large bribes from "wealthy Americans." All Westerners were wealthy by their standards. As soon as the border guards saw the letter on the emperor's personal stationery with his stamp and signature, they fell all over themselves to ingratiate themselves to us. We would see this same response many times. Just the sight of that piece of paper caused these people to tremble. Even though Haile Selassie was a relatively benign dictator, he had the power of life and death over anyone and they knew it. Most of these lower level officials could barely read or write, but they clearly recognized this very special document.

We were driving in the highland plateau region of Ethiopia. While it is called a plateau, it is far from flat. We would pass through brief rugged mountain sections and then the land would flatten out enough for it to be tilled. One of the most striking features of this rugged landscape was the extensive terracing of the hillsides. Where the land was good for growing crops, terraces were built up the side of the slopes until the terraces were only three or four feet wide. These were all built by hand as there was no powered equipment.

Ethiopian farmers raise a wide variety of grains and pulses (legumes used for food). These crops produce well in the volcanic soils, and the nitrogen fixing ability of legumes helps maintain soil fertility. Pulses are an excellent food source, as they provide an alternative source of protein when meat is not easily obtained. The most commonly grown and used pulses are horse beans, chickpeas, haricot beans, lentils, dry peas, and vetches. An important cereal grain crop is teff. It is native to Ethiopia

Terraced hillsides like these were common throughout our drive.

and is believed to have been cultivated for over 4,000 years. The seeds of this grass cereal are very tiny but exceptionally nutritious. Teff has more protein than wheat and is rich in iron that is easily absorbed. It also is gluten free.

Those two food crops provide the basic ingredients for Ethiopia's most common meal, wot and injera. Wot is a kind of stew whose foundation is built upon the pulse foods. It may be vegetable only or have meat added. It is also heavily spiced. Injera is fermented flatbread made with teff flour.

On the drive from Asmara to Addis Ababa, we encountered troops of baboons on several occasions. These are the gelada baboons found only in the highlands of Ethiopia. They have very heavy, shaggy fur coats to protect them against the cold highlands. These baboons live in the rugged mountains and can scamper up and down very steep cliffs with little difficulty. They come down out of the mountains to forage, often on a farmer's crops. A troop of baboons can do a lot of damage to a farmer's small plot of grain. We saw these troops as they traveled from their mountain homes to forage or returned with full bellies. They would usually stop a short distance from the road to watch us as we drove by. They did not seem to have much fear of humans. Farmers employed small boys to guard their fields using slings and rocks. The boys did very little damage to the baboons, but the farmers hoped the continual harassment would cause the baboons to seek their meals where they wouldn't have to dodge rocks.

In this region there are two growing seasons in three seasons. The heavy rainy season is called the *kiremt* rains. These are from June to September. Then the dry season called *bega* goes from October to January. The third season is the small rainy season called *belg,* from February to May. These two different rainy seasons allow the planting and harvesting of different kinds of crops. Some crops need lots of rain and are grown during the kiremt rains; others need less moisture and are grown during the belg season. The belg rains are also critical for providing rain to sustain grazing land for animals.

The first day's journey was quite pleasant. We passed many herds of goats and cattle, all accompanied by herders in long flowing garments. In the morning it was very cool. The elevation at Asmara was 7,300 feet, and from that altitude we climbed until we reached Addis Ababa at 8,300 feet. The countryside was really interesting. Wherever the ground was either level or could be terraced, it was cultivated. All of this cultivation was done using hand tools. The farmers were sometimes assisted by oxen pulling wooden plows with small metal blades at the tip. I had seen pictures of this kind of cultivation in history books, but did not realize how many people still lived using this method of agriculture. Around noon, we stopped in a grove of trees near a stream for lunch. Having traveled all morning on dirt and gravel, we eagerly headed for the stream. Don stopped us and warned us to be very careful to use plenty of soap and be very careful not to get any water in our mouth. We were to first take a cup of water from our supply, rinse our mouths, spit that water into a basin and save it for rinsing our faces after washing with soap and the stream water. The water in the stream was not to touch any of our vessels. This was our first lesson in how to prevent intestinal parasites and other diseases that were everywhere.

At the end of the first day we stopped by a stream for the night. We set up our tents and Lyda began preparing a meal for us. It was at this campsite that I had a life-changing experience. Most of us, as we grow into adulthood, latch onto a system of belief. Quite often this system seems to be fairly complete and seems neat and tidy. It appears to have few, if any, loose ends. A fair number of us, for various reasons, hold onto that system very tightly. I was one of those who held tightly to my system and believed it was the correct system. I learned, however, that I was really afraid to examine that system. I'm sure you've heard or read this quote before: "The unexamined life is not worth living." It is reported that Socrates said that at his trial for heresy. He was on trial for encouraging his students to challenge the accepted beliefs of the time and think for themselves. Before my trip to Ethiopia, had anyone asked me if I had really examined my beliefs, I would have said without hesitation, "Absolutely, and I am completely satisfied that this is the truth."

In order to understand how this adventure challenged my belief system, a brief sketch of my life as a child may be helpful. Our church, as well as the other two churches in our small town of 300, held Sunday morning and Sunday evening services as well as Wednesday night prayer meetings. Our family attended all of these services whenever possible. As conservative as this church was, my mother came from an even more conservative church background. Her father was a lay preacher in the Free Methodist Church. From my mother's beliefs and what I have heard from others, her father must have been of the "fire and brimstone" persuasion. My mother was a very loving, caring person, deeply religious and very devout. She would go out of her way to help anyone she saw in need. I never had any doubt of her love for me, my brothers, or my father. This is in contrast to how I experienced her sense of herself. It seemed that she was always in doubt as to whether she was good enough to go to heaven, where she was sure her mother and father were. We always had family prayers each night before going to bed. We all knelt on the floor and each one said a prayer, with my mother saying the last prayer. My strongest memory of these sessions was that Mother seemed to be desperate and pleading in her praying.

How all of this affected me is perhaps best illustrated by one strong childhood memory. On occasion, when I walked home from our one-room country school about a mile from our house, no one was in the house nor outside working. When this happened, my first thought was, "The rapture has come and all my family has been taken but me. I am left because I am not good enough to be with them in heaven." (The rapture is the belief held by some Christians that God will remove all Christians from Earth to heaven to protect them before a period of great horror on Earth.) As I grew older, my beliefs were moderated enough for me not to carry that childhood terror with me at all times. Yet, I still clung to a very tightly constrained religious belief system. With this background, it is not surprising that I arrived in Ethiopia carrying a very conservative and rather rigid belief system.

* * *

It sometimes takes a strong experience to crack a personal system. My experience in Ethiopia was my personal "crack in the egg" of my unexamined and tightly held belief system. Events open doors. It is up to us to walk through them. I thank God that I was given that opportunity and chose to walk through the door. My time in Ethiopia began a process of major transformation in my faith, all for the better.

While we were cleaning up, Lyda had opened her ingenious "chuck wagon" kitchen. The tailgate of the Land Rover was lowered to reveal a wooden box that fit exactly the width of the back of the Land Rover. It was about a foot deep and about three feet tall. It had a hinged lid that locked tight when closed and, miraculously, only allowed a small amount of road dust to penetrate. When opened, it was supported by chains to make a nice work area for food preparation. This cabinet contained everything she needed to prepare meals on the road. Lyda made us a nice lunch with bread, canned meat, and a salad with vegetables she had brought from Asmara.

The afternoon drive was much the same. We stopped at the one store with a gas pump where we filled our gas tanks and extra jerry cans and bought some bread and a few tins of meat. Whenever we stopped to eat, we left the empty tin cans by the roadside. I asked Don about this, as I thought we were littering. He told us to look carefully as we traveled to see what the people used to cook with. I soon saw that they used every piece of tin they could find in very clever ways. Sometimes they used the tins without modification; sometimes they created fairly elaborate utensils from tin cans. Clearly, used tin cans were a valuable resource for these people who did not need to be taught how to recycle. After the tin can was no longer useful as a vessel, it was turned into interesting decoration, actually folk art pieces.

One very clever invention I saw many times was a musical instrument called a *kalimba* or *mbira*; in English it is known as a thumb piano. It was usually made from an empty cigar box and pieces of metal umbrella ribs or bicycle spokes. The ribs were attached to the box in such a way that the user held the box with both hands and used his thumbs to pluck the

end of each rib. The ribs were cut to different lengths to create the notes of their five-tone music scale. When plucked, the ribs vibrated and the box acted much like the case of a violin or guitar to create a sound box. The effect was quite pleasing.[1]

1.   YouTube - Kalimba Mbira Sansa Likembe Thumb Piano Lamellaphone
http://www.youtube.com/watch?v=zXgPaxxqLVg

When we had our camp set up for the night, Don said, "Let's go down to the stream and wash the dust off." You can imagine what we looked like after travelling ten hours on dirt roads. All during the day, every time we stopped, even for a few minutes, a crowd would seem to appear from nowhere. Ethiopia is one of the most densely populated areas in the world. The United Nations report for 2005 gives a density of 186 people per square mile. This is for a country slightly less than twice the size of Texas (935,183 square miles) in which much of the land is uninhabitable due to the rugged mountainous terrain. When we went down to the stream to bathe, I saw that the banks of the stream were crowded with people: men, women, and children. All of them were curious about these strange people travelling through their land. I realized we would have no privacy, so I naively asked Don where we could get undressed and bathe without people everywhere watching us. Don said very casually, "It won't bother them, don't let it bother you." Don's casual response was the crack in my egg. For the first time in my life I stripped naked and bathed in front of an audience of strange men, women, and children. Don was right. It did not seem to bother them at all; although, I noticed some of the children thought it was pretty funny.

This simple event allowed me to begin examining what I had always believed to be true. I was taught that it was morally wrong for a man to see or be seen naked by a woman if you were not married to that woman. This moral prohibition of mine was as strong as many other beliefs I held to be immutable. Don was one of the strongest Christians I had ever met. Clearly he did not consider this wrong. The egg was cracked and could not be put back together. If this absolute belief was not true, how many of my other strongly held beliefs were also only cultural beliefs? This event allowed me to begin to open up to all of God's wondrous creation.

At the time, I did not realize what an impact this event would have on my spiritual growth. I imagine that if I had been pressed at that time, I would have considered my spiritual growth complete. That is how narrow my view of spirituality was before the crack in my egg. Only looking back have I been able to see how that event was pivotal in helping me to become more and more open to experiencing new things. I became willing to examine strongly held beliefs. I was willing to suspend judgment and listen to what, before this event, I would have called heretical or even atheistic. I learned to see, to feel, to *know* that God, by whatever name he was called, or no name, was literally everywhere and in everything. I was able to experience God's spirit in events, in places, and with people doing things I never knew were spiritual. My spirituality has become much deeper and my faith much more profound. I know without question that as long as I live I will have opportunities for continuing spiritual growth.

The rest of the trip to Addis Ababa was largely uneventful. We had driven over seven hundred miles of dirt and gravel road in two days and had climbed from 7,300 feet to 8,300 feet elevation. The only effect of the elevation that I noticed was that I tired more easily. The entire first day we saw no other vehicles moving on the road.

Quite a distance from Addis, we began to see donkeys and horses with large bundles of sticks tied to their backs. Occasionally there would be a horse- or donkey-drawn two-wheel cart piled high with sticks. It seemed a wonder these carts did not tip over on the many bumps in the road. Nearer to the city, we saw people, mostly women, carrying large bundles of sticks on the tops of their heads. All of this was to bring wood for fires in the city. Most of these sticks were no bigger than a broomstick and many were much smaller. As the population of Ethiopia has exploded, the once well-forested country has been stripped of trees to provide firewood and building material. This deforestation is a primary cause of the severe droughts and famine the country has suffered. As we got nearer the city we saw more and more people and actually started seeing vehicle traffic. We had to slow down mostly because of the number of people and animals in the road.

The Italian occupation has left its imprint on the language of Ethiopia, Amharic. Perhaps the most common word that non-Ethiopians are likely to hear and hear very often is *ferengi*, which means foreigner or stranger in Italian. As we neared the city and the heavy traffic of people and animals forced us to drive very slowly, children would shout out "ferengi, ferengi" as soon as they saw us. When we were moving away from the children they sometimes shouted "Ciao," the Italian good-bye.

We quickly learned the Amharic greeting, *tanayistill-ing*, which literally means "May God give you health." We also heard *salam* as a greeting, which is adapted from the Arabic greeting, "Salaam," meaning peace, or "Salaam alaikum," which is "peace to you." The incorporation of these Arabic words is due to the long history of Muslim influence in Ethiopia.

The pitiful condition of most of the people, especially the children, was all too evident. They were all very thin, some emaciated, and their clothing was just rags. A lot of them had visible open sores that were covered with flies. Many of the very small children had distended bellies, telling of extreme mal-nutrition. The plight of these children was heartbreaking. We saw hundreds, but there were many thousands we did not see. The roadsides were lined with beggars only partly due to the extreme poverty. Begging is a cultural institution that carries no stigma for the one begging. The Coptic Church supports the practice by teaching the people that giving something to a beg-gar assures a blessing from heaven. On the outskirts of Addis Ababa the road was still dirt and gravel. We were well into the city before it became paved. The area where the American mis-sion and school were located was fairly nice but side streets were still dirt. Fortunately we arrived at the mission in short order.

This is typical of the kinds of roads and deep ruts we
encountered on the drive down to Gambela.

CHAPTER FOUR

8,000 FEET TO 600:
OUR DRIVE FROM ADDIS ABABA
TO GAMBELA

We spent a couple of days in Addis resting and preparing for the drive down to Gambela. Don took us to a restaurant for a traditional Ethiopian dinner, wot and injera. We sat on rugs on the floor around a large, tightly woven basket about twenty inches wide, shaped something like a Chinese wok. The servers brought large sheets of injera and lined the basket with several of these. Injera is made from a local grass seed called teff. The sheets of injera look like very thin sheets of foam rubber. They are cooked on a flat grill much like pancakes. The injera mix is made the day before and left to ferment. The mix is very thin and when poured on the grill spreads out quickly. It is cooked only on one side and as soon as the little bubbles form, it is ready. It doesn't get browned. Injera by itself tastes sour from the fermentation. Once the basket is lined with injera, the wot is scooped into the middle of the basket. Everyone tears off a piece of injera and scoops up some wot to eat. Each course gets progressively hotter with spice. Don told us, "You gauge how good the meal is by how many handkerchiefs it takes to get through the meal." A really good meal is a three- or four-handkerchief meal. Our dinner was at least a five-handkerchief meal. Wot is a kind of stew made with any available meat. Traditionally the meal starts with two or three vegetable courses, each one a little spicier, and then meat courses. They will always have two or three courses of chicken, goat, lamb, or sausage. The meal was wonderful. Don had warned us to eat only a little of each course or we wouldn't make it through the meal. He was right.

Don ordered Ethiopian beer to drink with the meal. This was another shattering of my "egg." I had been raised to believe that any alcoholic drink was the drink of the devil and no good Christian would ever drink it! Here again was a man and wife who had devoted their lives to serving Christ—certainly a strong Christian couple—and they were drinking beer and ordered it for us. I had wondered what we would do for something to drink with our meal. We had been told that it was unsafe to drink any water, coffee, or tea anyplace in Ethiopia. Bottled water was also unsafe unless you bought it in sealed cases as they did for the mission. Often places that sold individual bottled water would take the empty bottles and refill them with tap water. The mission bought water in cases and they had a purifier. If neither of those were available, you boiled the water for fifteen minutes. If that wasn't possible, you could add some chlorine to the water and let it sit for a while. Because of the alcohol in beer and wine, these were the only safe drinks you could buy by the bottle. Even bottled soda was not considered safe. Canned soda was not available. Once more I was shown that you must use your head and not rely on predetermined absolutes.

The next day I was helping the driver of one of the trucks that was to take our gear to Gambela. He spoke pretty good English and asked me where we were going. I told him we were going down to Gambela to help Dr. McClure build a new mission station on the Gilo River. He looked at me kind of strangely and then said, "That is where the black people live!" This man, while not black as coal, was as dark as a piece of dark walnut. I was shocked, but said nothing. Clearly I wasn't the only one with preconceived ideas! The highland people are descended from people who have the same genetic heritage as people from India and other Near Eastern people. Most of the highland people have very dark skin but their facial features are not Negroid.

This encounter brought back an experience I had while a student at Sterling College in the 1950s. One summer I decided to sell World Book Encyclopedias to earn money for school. (As a money-making venture, it was a total loss!) Another student at Sterling chose to do the same thing. Peter was from Ethiopia and had come to Sterling because it was a strong Christian school. He and I had become friends and we thought selling World Books was worth a try. Peter had stressed that while he was born and raised in Ethiopia, he was really Greek. At the time, I did not understand why this was so important to him. We went together to Topeka, Kansas, for the training class to sell World Books. At lunch on the first day we went to eat at a nearby restaurant. We walked in and sat down in a booth. After a long wait I noticed that other people, who had come in after us, were being served. I got up and asked to see the manager. When I asked him why we were being ignored, he said, "I can serve you but not the man who is with you." I was shocked and suddenly understood. This was my first personal experience of our country's discrimination against black people. I was barely able to contain my anger, but I did. I went back and had to ask my friend, Peter, to come with me. When we got outside, I explained with tears in my eyes what had happened. Peter, too, was naturally very angry. It took me a while to realize that his anger was not at being discriminated against, it was because he had been mistaken for a "black" person! Peter's skin also was the color of walnut. These two incidents show how deep the racial prejudice is in Ethiopia, which is the root of much of the atrocities still continuing there.

During our brief stay in Addis Ababa we had the opportunity to be introduced to one of Ethiopia's infamous wild animals, the spotted hyena or laughing hyena. As a child I recall reading about hyenas and seeing their pictures in *National Geographic* magazine. Their long front legs, barrel shaped bodies, and squat hind legs gave them a very ungainly appearance. I knew very little about these animals before going to Ethiopia. Here, I would learn a great deal about these strange creatures. Our first encounter with them was in Addis Ababa when we were being driven back to the mission station at night. Suddenly I saw gleaming yellow eyes that seemed to shine like beacons staring right at us. I was quickly told that those were the infamous spotted hyenas. They were prowling the streets of Addis Ababa, the capital city, just as if they owned the place. In fact, that is almost true.

Hyenas are scavengers, and they much prefer easy meals to ones they must work for. They have become the garbage disposal agents for all of the cities and towns in Ethiopia where there was no public garbage collection and only very little private collection. Hyenas were regarded as a necessary evil. The people needed them to prevent garbage and the bodies of dead animals from becoming a serious problem. In most towns and small cities, hyenas owned the towns at night. It was unsafe to be out at night. While hyenas prefer to pick up whatever they can find, they will also grab an easy meal when it presents itself. They usually do not bother adults, unless they are alone. Children were warned, "Do not go out at night or you may end up in the hyena's belly." Not an idle warning!

The fearsome power of the hyena's enormous jaws is legendary. We were told that on one occasion a driver of a Land Rover saw a hyena on the road and chased it in an effort to run it over. As the Land Rover got close, the hyena turned on the jeep and ripped a tire off the Land Rover with those powerful jaws while it was still moving.

* * *

Since ascending the steep escarpment between Massawa and Asmara, we had been driving on what is called the Highland

Plateau. On this next part of our drive we would be descending the western slope. This is the region where the rivers and streams gather the heavy rainfall of the monsoon season and deliver that water to the Nile River. The western plateau of Ethiopia covers almost half of the country. While it is called a plateau, it is far from flat. This very rugged land is the source of the many rivers and streams that feed into the Nile River. The most famous and the one that brings the most water to the Nile is the Blue Nile that originates in Lake Tana in northwestern Ethiopia; however, there are many other rivers and streams that feed the Nile. Two of those are the Baro River and the Gilo River. Gambela is on the Baro, and the new mission station we would build was on the Gilo.

The Nile River is the longest river in the world at 4,130 miles long. The length is continually challenged as explorers push deeper and higher for the first trickles of water. It has two main branches: the White Nile originating in Central Africa and the Blue Nile originating in Ethiopia. Ninety percent of the water in the Nile comes from Ethiopia's western plateau. The western plateau has a distinct dry season from mid-September to June. When the monsoon rains blow over the Indian Ocean and bring the mois-ture-laden air up over the plateau, the air cools and the moisture condenses and falls in torrential rains from mid-June to September.

The western slope descends in a series of three steps. The first step begins not too far from Addis and descends quite steeply to a more gradual slope that continues until the next step. These steps divide the slope into three roughly equal sec-tions. The last step brings you down to the flat lowlands of the

Nile plain. Because of the heavy rainfall, this whole rugged region is deeply eroded. It is difficult to describe just how rugged this region is. The Blue Ridge Mountains are perhaps the closest example of the terrain. You have to imagine them with almost no valleys and only a few dirt roads to cross them.

The day after our Ethiopian meal we rose early to make the 400-mile trip from Addis Ababa to Gambela. Don wanted to make sure we could get there before dark. It was not safe to stop at night over much of the route without armed guards. This road was much worse than our road from Asmara. This road was all dirt and heavily used by all-wheel-drive freight trucks even during the rainy season. Fortunately this was the dry season. The road was cut for miles by huge deep ruts made by the trucks. The only way we could prevent our Land Rovers from getting hung up on the high center hump was to drive with two wheels on the hump and two in the rut. When you needed to drive in the opposite rut you had to quickly make the vehicle jump over the hump. After a couple of times with the other fellows trying to drive in the ruts and getting hung up, Don asked me, as the only one with off-road driving experience, to drive and to ford the many streams we crossed with no bridges. When we got hung up on a rut, we would have to get picks and shovels, prop up one side with logs and dig out from under the vehicle until we could again get traction. This took a lot of time. Since Don was in front of us and he never got hung up, we could also use that Land Rover to help get the other one moving.

The road was often quite steep as well. We were descending from over 8,000 feet down to less than 1,000 on the upper Nile tributaries. Whenever we passed small villages, Don sped up to barely controllable speeds. He told me not to stop, no matter what, because of the risk of being held up by thugs. Several times I was afraid we would hit someone or something, but I stayed right behind him and we passed safely. I knew God had to be with us or we could not have made it. We did reach Gambela just before dark. What a trip! We all breathed a sigh of relief and thanked God for our safe passage.

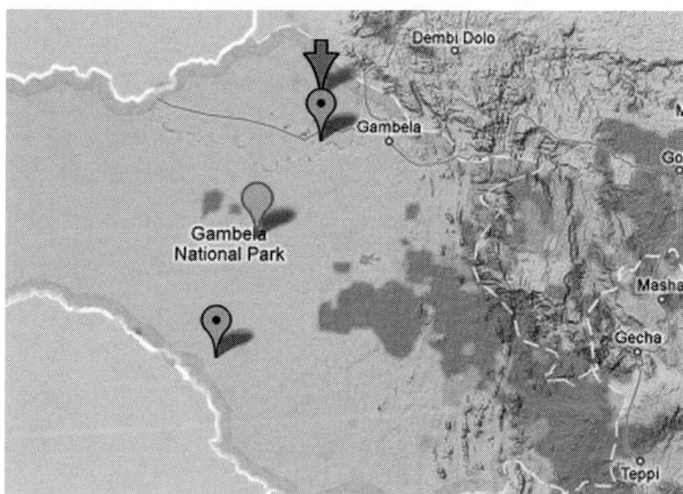

Google terrain map of the Gambela Region.

The upper pin marks the approximate location of the Pokwo mission station. The lower pin is where I believe the Gilo River station was located.

These are typical of the houses built by the Anuak.

CHAPTER FIVE

FLIGHT TO THE GILO ROVER: SETTING UP CAMP

After we arrived at Gambela, Don arranged for a boat to take us down river to Pokwo, the mission at Gambela. We would have a few days there to get ready before flying over to the Gilo River. At the mission we met our first Anuaks. This was the local tribe we would be with for the next eight months. Don had worked with this tribe for quite a while and spoke the language fluently. The Anuak are mostly agricultural. They grow corn and several other vegetables including manioc. They also have some chickens for meat and eggs. They raise a few goats for meat and milk. They live on the river so they also are able to get fish. Overall they have a fairly healthy diet. If it were not for the many endemic diseases and unsanitary living conditions, their lives would be primitive but quite healthy.

The Anuak live in round houses made from a frame of tree limbs stuck in the ground and lashed together using the long elephant grass for string. Once the frame is up, they cover the roof with a thick grass thatch of the same elephant grass. It is well named, as you have to be as tall as an elephant to see over it. It is seven or eight feet tall when it matures and makes a watertight roof. It also makes a great home for a variety of insects, including scorpions. After the roof is put on, the space between the logs that hold up the roof is filled with smaller sticks woven together with twigs until it is completely filled. They leave an opening for a door, but there are no window openings. These houses are used for sleeping, storage, and shelter from the rainy season. When the walls are filled, the women usually plaster those walls with mud and make a hard mud floor that is surprisingly durable if it does not get wet. Of course, it is easy to repair with a little water and smoothing if it does get wet. The women also smooth the area in front of the houses where they grind corn or manioc, cook, and prepare meals. The Anuak people have had little genetic mixing with lighter skinned people from Europe or Asia, so their skin is as black as you can imagine. I have rarely seen a black person in the United States with skin that dark. The men usually wear shorts that are sometimes so ragged they barely hold together. The men also have armbands made from a variety of things, but ivory and brass are especially treasured. Women wear only a small apron or, sometimes, for special occasions they wear Western style smock-like dresses, if they have them.

Until the age of puberty, the children wear no clothing. Don told us that on their first furlough home, he and Lyda were quite concerned how their two young children, who had lived only with the Anuaks, would do. The oldest, a girl, was old enough to go to school. When she got home after her first day at school she seemed okay. They asked her how she liked it, and in typical young child style she said, "Fine." So Don, trying to get her to talk about it a little more, asked her how many boys and girls were in her class. She said, "I don't know." Don asked how it was that she did not know how many boys and girls there were. She looked at him as if he had lost his mind and answered, "They all had clothes on!"

As soon as an Anuak infant gets his two front teeth, they are removed. The Anuaks say that this is to keep the child from evil spirits. Since mothers often nurse their children until age three, it makes sense to remove those teeth. Since removing the teeth is for the purpose of keeping evil spirits away, it is therefore necessary to also remove the permanent two front teeth when they come in. This makes it very difficult for non-Anuaks to speak the language and make the same sounds, partially created by missing teeth!

At puberty, boys go through an extensive initiation ritual that gives them status as an adult man. A significant part of that ritual is the process of scarification. This is the creation of several rows of dot-like scars on their foreheads. These scars are distinctive for each tribe. The Dinka, Nuer, and Anuaks are related linguistically, and each uses a different scarification that marks them as members of that tribe. To make the scars, a sharp knife is used to make a small incision and ashes are rubbed in it to make the bump. Infection is infrequent because they use fire to sterilize the knife and the ashes are fresh from the same fire. After puberty, girls cover their genitals, at least with a small apron. Boys may or may not, but usually they acquire some form of bottom covering.

The Anuaks have a strong belief in a higher power. The word they use to name the highest of these powers is "Jwok." The Gospel song often sung by youth as a round, "Praise Ye the Lord, Hallelujah," is translated (my spelling) "Warr ninga Jowk Allaluia." Many powerful things are considered to have Jwok, such as cobras, crocodiles, some especially large trees, the river, and the village leader. These are only a few of the things that have Jwok. Jwok has both positive and negative influence. I doubt if anyone not born and raised in Anuak culture really has a good understanding of what Jwok really means or implies.

A week's stay at the Pokwo mission helped us recuperate from the exhausting road trip we had just completed and get ready to move our stuff to the Gilo River. We had to pack everything we would need for at least an eight-month stay without supplies coming in. Don did not know whether they would be able to get the Missionary Aviation Fellowship (MAF) plane from the Sudan to come back again after this time. There was no way to get anything to the new mission site except by someone carrying it sixty miles through the bush. We packed canned food, tents, cots, mosquito nets, and nylon screens to screen in the house we were to build. We had to pack any tools we would need: axes, saws, shovels, pickaxes, mattocks, etc. It was exciting and a little daunting to realize that we would be camping out in the African bush for at least six months.

A Cessna 172 on floats owned by the Missionary Aviation Fellowship and based in Sudan would be used to fly us to the Gilo. The plane would load at the Pokwo mission and fly to the new Gilo River site. Don had flown with the pilot earlier to scout out the site, so the pilot knew it well. The Gilo River site was approximately sixty miles by air from the Pokwo mission, so it was a short flight. When the day arrived we were all excited. The plane arrived early in the morning. Don said he wanted me to fly in with him on the first flight with just a few supplies. He said the plane would make several trips the first day but might not get all we needed until the next day. I was really excited about flying in a small plane again. I had not flown in a small plane since I flew as a mechanic in Alaska. Don gave me the privilege of flying in the front seat next to the pilot. Since it was such a short flight we flew quite low and I could see really well. It was just like a National Geographic film only better; I was there. I got to see lots of animals. There was a herd of giraffes, a small herd of elephants, some zebras, and lots of antelope. I had hoped for a glimpse of the notorious water buffalo but that was not to be. The flight seemed to be over before it began. All too soon, the pilot pointed ahead and said, "There is the Gilo River."

The river was only about one hundred feet wide, much smaller than I expected, but had a pretty swift current. This did not concern our pilot. The pilot circled a nearby Anuak village and then made several low passes to be sure there were neither obstructions nor canoes in the river. He banked sharply and brought the plane into a perfect upstream landing. After landing, he taxied back around to come upstream to the landing area. There were Anuaks on the bank ready to grab the wingtip and pull us over to the bank and makeshift dock of tied-together, dugout canoes. The high wing of the Cessna made it easy to load and unload from a dock. I was in awe! Here I was literally in the middle of the African bush surrounded by nothing but the natural world the way God made it. No towns or roads anywhere, only the trails used by the Anuaks and the animals. No whites except Don, the pilot, and myself. I loved it! I did not have long to revel in the wonder of this adventure. We quickly unloaded the plane so the pilot could return for another load. After the other boys and Lyda flew in, all the seats but the pilot's would be removed to haul more of our equipment each load. Immediately after the plane took off, Don said, "We need to get this area cleared for our campsite." Don directed the work while the local Anuaks and I got busy with axes, mattocks, picks, and shovels. We removed brush, the smaller trees, and some large termite hills. We left the larger trees for shade and a place to hang things.

I had seen pictures of termite hills in films and TV shows, but until I stood next to one I had no idea how big they were. They were truly a marvel of creation. Tiny little termites create huge mounds, many over six feet tall and more than thirty feet across at the base. The mounds were almost like cement. The termites build them from dirt and spit. What a lovely thought! There were lots of them in the area where we were building the new mission station. There would be a termite hill every twenty or thirty feet or less, and all of them had to be

Imagine chopping one of these down every twenty feet with only hand tools. The mud mixed with termite saliva is as hard as a brick.

removed. I grabbed a shovel and thought I would just shove it in and start shoveling the hill down. When I swung the shovel into the termite hill, it rang like a bell and gave my shoulders and hands quite a jolt. The only way to dig them down was with a pickaxe. Now I knew why we brought so many. In addition to being tough as cement to break up, the termite hills also harbored another nasty surprise. They were the preferred home of the spitting cobra! So to take down one of these hills, you had to chop it down with a pickaxe while watching carefully for cobras that might come out fighting mad at what you are doing to their home. You, of course, had to be sure you were not bitten and also prevent them from spitting their venom in your eyes. My training this first day on termite hills would prove to be invaluable in just a few days. Little did I know just how valuable!

As soon as we got the campsite cleared, Don wanted to show me where the airstrip was to be located. Knowing that I had been a helicopter mechanic in the army and had flown a lot in Alaska, he wanted my opinion about the site. One end of the runway would be near the river, the other end was past where our camp was set up. The runway would be 300 feet wide by 3,000 feet long. Don said he wanted it to be large enough for a DC3 cargo plane to land and take off. He said he was told the DC3 needed a minimum of 2,500 feet. I thought the layout looked really good. I especially liked the fact that one end was near the river. We could cut the trees between the river and runway and allow an airplane to make a low approach over the water. That would increase the effective length of the runway.

The plane kept making trips throughout the day bringing supplies and one person each trip. Charlie, one of our group, had gotten a bad cut on his leg while helping with the loading and would have to stay at the Pokwo mission until it healed. By the middle of the afternoon, we had a nice camp cleared, with several large trees to provide shade. Don had directed the Anuaks to weave a fence made of the tall elephant grass to enclose the mound of "stuff" that we were bringing to the camp. He said if we didn't do this, by morning all that would be left would be a dust pile, as the Anuaks considered anything left lying on the ground fair game for the finder. The only trace left of your stuff might be when an Anuak came along the trail carrying a cup made from a Spam can! On the next to last flight, Don flew back with the pilot to see how the move was coming along. When the plane returned, Don wasn't with it and asked that Lyda return. They would stay at the mission until the next day as he wasn't feeling well. He sent instructions for us and our Anuak cook, Omut, on how to set up camp, secure the stored goods, and get our cots and mosquito nets arranged. He would see us in the morning, he said.

Right after we finished getting everything ready, a local Anuak brought in a huge freshly caught Nile perch. It must have weighed at least fifty pounds. They are as big as the Florida Keys' grouper. So we had freshly grilled Nile perch for our first meal at the camp. We put chunks of fish on the end of a stick like a hot dog and cooked it over the open fire. It was absolutely delicious. You could not have had better fish in the finest restaurant. Fish-on-a-stick made us a perfect meal for our first night at the camp. We cleaned up the camp and our few eating utensils. Then we took baths in the river and made sure we watched for crocodiles while bathing. The Anuaks said they were rarely seen in this part of the river because the current was too swift, but we thought it was still a good idea to be watchful. We were all tired from a long, busy day and fell right to sleep under the stars with a lullaby of mosquitoes humming around the mosquito nets covering each cot. Getting into the cots and keeping the mosquito nets completely sealed by the ground cloths was quite a gymnastic exercise, but we soon learned how or stayed up swatting mosquitoes all night.

Google terrain map of where I believe the
Gilo River station was located.

The Anuak village to the right of center has moved to the opposite side of the river from when we were there, probably to have easier access to the clinic and other facilities. You can see a bend in a road at the far right. Of course, there were no roads when we were there. I imagine the government built the road to have access to the landing strip, which I am sure was heavily used during the Sudan conflict. You can see a partially cleared strip running diagonally away from the bend in the river. This is exactly the position of the airstrip we built. Now it has been allowed to be taken over by grass and trees. The station was closed to foreigners before the Sudan conflict got really bad and has never been allowed to reopen.

CHAPTER SIX

A CRYPTIC MESSAGE FOR DAVE

The next morning Dave, Chuck, and I were up at sunrise and had breakfast that our cook, Omut, made to surprise us. He made pancakes with canned syrup and fried Spam. It was delicious and just what we needed to start our busy day. We immediately began working on a screened covered shelter that we planned to use as a place to relax and eat free of flies until Don got his house built. While the others worked on the shelter, I began building our "sanitary" facilities. I dug a trench latrine and built a log "throne" to sit on. It even had a place for the toilet paper roll and a backrest! I was pretty proud of my creation. Fortunately, Don had shipped in bags of lime to use with dirt to help keep flies down. I then had the Anuaks build a woven grass privacy fence with a blind entrance. We had an old towel that you were to hang on the post by the entrance to signal "occupied." It worked quite well. My next project was a stand to hold the washbasin with a place for soap and a small mirror hanging over the basin. It was a three-legged stand made from small branches. It sure beat having to sit on the ground to wash up.

While all this was going on we kept listening for the sound of the airplane. By mid-morning when we had not heard anything, we began to get a little anxious. By noon when we still had not heard anything we tried to think of positive scenarios, rather than the nagging fears that "something awful" had happened. Since I had some experience with small airplanes, I suggested several possible events that could cause a delay of arrival of the airplane. First, I said that small mechanical problems are always cropping up and must be fixed before the airplane can fly. Also I knew that the pilot had to go back to the Sudan to refuel and there might have been some problem causing a delay with the refueling. We clung to these positive scenarios as the day wore on until we knew that it was too late for a plane to arrive. We cleaned up, had a light supper, and by dark were in our cots, trying to sleep. Since we had been physically working pretty hard, eventually we fell into a sound sleep and were awakened by the sun hitting our cots.

We got up and had a quick breakfast of cereal and canned milk. Each of us tried to find useful things to do while we again waited for the sound of the airplane arriving. The second day was the same as the first: no comforting sound of an airplane. We occupied ourselves with improving the camp to keep from worrying. As the day progressed, we found ourselves getting more and more anxious. We struggled to maintain a positive attitude. In mid-afternoon, Dave, Chuck, and I got together, and someone said, "You know, we haven't joined to-gether in prayer about this!" We did and, as always, at least for me, felt much calmer, and I truly felt and believed that every-thing would be all right. I felt strongly that we would be okay.

We had a pleasant, relaxed evening meal that Omut cooked for us and began to enjoy the efforts we had put in to make our camp comfortable and pleasant. We all slept well and had a pleasant if simple breakfast of coffee, cereal, and dried milk. One of the fellows preferred chocolate milk, so he tried mixing powdered milk and powdered chocolate with a little sugar. We all tried it and pronounced it, if not delicious, at least drinkable. Again the time for an early arrival of the plane passed, but we were learning quite well to handle the disap-pointment. Around ten o'clock we heard the sound we had all been anxiously awaiting, the unmistakable whine of an airplane engine. We shouted with relief and joy! Someone shouted, "Da plane, da plane!" and we all broke up with laughter and relief.

As the plane got closer and we could see it, two things immediately alerted us. First, it was much too high to be pre-paring to land. Second, I saw that the airplane did not have the floats attached that would allow it to land on the river. I imme-diately ran to the radio (receive only) that Don had shown me how to use to tune in aircraft frequencies. I turned it on, the vol-ume up, but all I could hear was static. I frantically begin dialing up and down the frequencies and suddenly I heard something not static. I carefully tried to tune in that sound. This was not a very accurate tuner and certainly not digital. Finally I got it loud and clear. This is what I heard: "Message to Dave, message to Dave, do not hunt, do not leave camp, a message will follow in five days." This message was repeated three times and as the airplane circled overhead, the pilot said, "If you hear this message, three of you wave your shirts at the same time." We grabbed our shirts and waved them and we saw the airplane wiggle its wings, indicating the pilot saw us. I rushed back to the radio hoping for more, but that was it. The message repeated three more times. The pilot said, "God be with you," and the airplane flew away toward the Sudan.

We immediately gathered together to discuss what this meant. We had very little to go on. The facts were few and the message very cryptic. No floatplane came so we concluded that something happened to prevent its return. "A message will follow in five days." I knew that the Pokwo was about sixty miles overland through the bush. I believed this message meant that someone was going to walk from the mission here, and that it would take about five days. This sounded about right to me, as I did not think there was any direct trail. Most trails follow the rivers. I did not know nor could we come up with a logical reason why the pilot could not give us any more information than he did. I did know that in the States pilots are not supposed to transmit on the radio "blind," that is, without a known ground station or another aircraft. The idea is that the use of the radio is strictly supposed to be two-way unless the aircraft declares an emergency. I also knew from talking with a missionary pilot that both Ethiopia and the Sudan were very strict about following the rules to the letter.

I suggested that we needed a plan of action based on what we did know and supplemented by what we hoped were intelligent guesses. The others all agreed. We decided the first part of the message was clear enough. We would not hunt nor leave the camp. This is when our planning got fuzzy. I said that in order for people or supplies to get here, other than by walking, we needed to get started on building the airstrip. I also thought that since the airstrip was right beside our camp that this still adhered to the spirit of the message of staying in camp. The others were not so sure. I said we also needed something productive to do, instead of just worrying. Further discussion did not seem to produce any consensus. I asked for us to take a break and each of us think and pray about it. Then at lunch we would see what we could agree on.

For some time, I had developed the practice of quiet meditation to relax and clear my mind. Often after doing so, a problem would become clear or a plan of action would suggest itself. After meditating on our problem for a time, an idea came to me. On the first day of our arrival, Don had shown me where he planned to build the airstrip. I knew that one end would be very near the river. I knew that it was to be 300 feet wide and 3,000 feet in length. I did not know for sure where the end of the airstrip away from the river would be, but I guessed it would be very near our campsite or perhaps a bit beyond. So the idea that came to me was this: we could start work on the end of the airstrip near the camp and therefore not really leave the campsite.

When I told the others my idea at lunch they all enthusiastically agreed we could and should do this. That afternoon we began scouting out where we thought the airstrip would be. We went to the river end first. We wanted some kind of landmark that we could see and then lay a straight line to it. When we got near the river and also near where I remembered Don showing me the end of the airstrip should be, I noticed there was a tall tree right on the bank of the river with an unusual shape. If you looked just right, it looked like it could be a person bowing toward where the airstrip would be. When I saw this tree, I immediately thought of what Don had said about the Anuaks and the word Jwok. To the Anuak, many things were Jwok, especially something different. Big trees could be Jwok. I felt that this tree was Jwok, or at least a sign from God for us. It helped reassure me that we were indeed doing the right thing, and this was the exact place to mark the river end of the airstrip.

I pointed out the tree to Chuck and Dave and said, "I think that is about where the end and edge of the airstrip should be." I told them no more about what I saw and felt. When they looked at the tree, they noted its unusual features and said it would be a good landmark. I asked them both to look at the tree again and see if they saw anything other than it was odd or unusual. Chuck said, "Yes, it looks a little like a tall old man." Then Dave said, "I can see that, and it looks like he's bending over toward us." I then told them what I had seen and that I thought this was our Jwok. I wasn't sure what their reaction would be, but they both agreed that was our Jwok tree!

I asked one of them to stay near the tree and sent the other up near our camp where I would pace toward him for 1,000 paces. I knew one of my paces was close to three feet. Chuck was near the camp and found an old abandoned termite hill he could climb on to see better. I also wanted them to signal me to go left or right if I wasn't walking close to a straight line. Of course, I also had to dodge termite hills and trees. With our Jwok tree to guide us, I paced off 1,000 paces and then added fifty more to be sure. Just as I had guessed, that brought the end of the airstrip to just a little beyond the campsite. There was another tall tree near this end that we could use for a marker on the campsite end of the airstrip. I then paced off the width of the airstrip, and we marked that edge as well. We now had something positive to do, and we all felt much better. That evening during our supper meal, Dave, Chuck, and I discussed how we would begin. We developed a tentative plan of action. We would first clear all the brush and small trees in a line at the camp end of the airstrip. We would then widen that line to about fifty feet. After that, we would cut down all the trees in that fifty-foot strip, then chop down the termite hills and dig out the tree stumps. If it sounds like a lot of work, you're right, it was a lot of hard work, but it was just what we needed to keep us busy and feeling good about accomplishing a job that needed to be done.

I had had some training in survival concepts in the army in preparation for our deployment to the Arctic slope of northern Alaska. So we decided we needed to take a look at our resources. We had a pretty good supply of canned vegetables and some canned meat, especially Spam. We later learned that Spam could be used in ways we never would have imagined. We could get fish from the Anuaks who trapped fish in a large trap woven from small branches or used their fish spears to spear larger fish like the delicious Nile Perch. During the weeks to come, we learned that the Anuaks also had a few chickens, so we could occasional buy a chicken to cook or some fresh eggs. The only local vegetable we could get was manioc, a very starchy tuber that the Anuaks had in abundance. It made a very good substitute for potatoes. Fortunately, Omot knew several different ways to prepare it, so we didn't get too bored with it. So we believed our food needs would be taken care of.

One of the items that came over on the plane that first day was a gravity flow ceramic water filter, and this proved to be very vital. Without it we would have had to boil all our drinking water. We also had canvas water bags that cooled the water as it seeped through the bag by evaporation. We had some large plastic water storage containers that we could let fill with filtered water during the day and overnight, as the filter was rather slow flowing. We filled two of the canvas bags each morning and again after lunch, so we could take them wherever we were working and hang them from a tree branch.

We had a small supply of potassium permanganate pills that we could use in an emergency to sterilize water. These were what we used to wash the few fresh leafy vegetables that the Anuaks brought us.

We were fortunate that it was not the rainy season, so we had plenty of time to build a thatched-roof sleeping hut. We left a gap between the roof and the lower stick wall that was just the width we needed for our screened window. Fortunately a roll of nylon screening had been among the loads of goods that first day. Dave and Chuck attached the nylon screen all the way around the hut. While they were doing that, I found a wooden crate that I took apart to build a frame for our screen door. By the end of the day, our sleeping hut was completed and secure.

We were very fortunate with the weather. Even though we were only about seven degrees north of the equator, the temperatures ranged from the upper 80s to the mid-90s most of the time. There were probably a few days that touched 100 degrees but not many. It was probably the amount of vegetation that helped keep the temperature reasonable. There was a nice breeze almost all the time. As these Upper Nile lowlands heated up during the day, the western slope of Ethiopia created a natural draft effect, sucking the hot air up that slope and giving us a nice breeze.

At night as we lay in our cots with the mosquito nets around us, we had quite a symphony to sing us to sleep. There was the ever-present singing of mosquitoes, angry that they couldn't get at all that delicious blood inside our nets. We would often hear the distant calls of monkeys or baboons warning the troop of some danger. Perhaps there was a leopard nearby or pack of hyenas. Sometimes we could hear the distant maniacal howling laugh of a hyena. It was a very creepy sound, especially at night with nothing but a thin, fragile net between you and that entire wilderness!

One night a few days after we got to the Gilo, before we had fallen asleep, we heard a sound that sent chills up our spines. It was a deep, guttural, very loud cough. We all said at the same time, "What was that?" We forgot about sleep. We all sat up in our cots and listened. The same coughing sound repeated periodically. At first, when the sound repeated, it was still quite loud. Then, after a bit, it began to grow fainter, which we believed meant that whatever was making the sound was moving away from us. We got little sleep that night. The next morning we described what we heard to Omot and asked him if he knew what it was. Omot chuckled and said that was a pride of lions hunting. The cough we heard was the sound of members of the pride keeping track of each other. This was not comforting news.

One time at night, we heard a very loud snort and the sound of pounding hooves running away. The next morning we saw clear hoof prints and dung on the airstrip near our camp. A herd of water buffalo had apparently come upwind toward our camp. Only when they got close did they pick up our scent, which caused them to run away. The name water buffalo does not sound like an animal to be concerned about, but the African water buffalo is one of the most dangerous wild animals in Africa. It's right up there with the king of beasts, the lion. It is very territorial and is not afraid of anything. We rarely heard the trumpeting of an elephant warning off an intruder. Not a symphony that I would have chosen to hear in just that way, but nevertheless a truly wondrous experience. The hard physical work we were doing helped us to fall quickly asleep at night, in spite of the nightly concerts.

* * *

The three of us would usually be joined by two or three Anuaks when they learned what we were doing. We found that we could completely clear a twenty-foot strip the width of the airstrip in about three days, depending on how many big trees and termite hills we encountered. It had been five days since the "Message to Dave!" and we had cleared a fifty-foot long area the width of the airstrip. It was still very rough, but we had removed all trees, dug out the stumps, and chopped all termite hills down to ground level. We felt pretty good about our accomplishment. We always quit work for a substantial lunch and a short rest period after lunch. We had just finished lunch when we heard the Anuaks shouting. Shortly after that, an Anuak who was not a local walked into camp. He had much newer, cleaner clothes, much like our own, and greeted us in English. He said, "Hello Dave, I have a message for you." He then handed me an envelope with my name on it.

It was quite a long letter addressed to all of us. I asked the others if they wanted me to read it out loud or if they wanted to wait and read it themselves. They wanted me to read it, so I did. The highlight was Don had undulant fever, a disease something like malaria requiring extensive bed rest and probably months for full recuperation. The other one of our group, Charlie, who had cut his leg the day we flew in, would not be able to come until his cut, now infected, was fully healed. The floatplane that was based in Sudan had been prohibited by the Sudanese government from returning to Ethiopia. This was due to the growing conflict between Sudan and Ethiopia. Just as I thought, we would need to have the airstrip completed before supplies and people could come in.

Don confirmed in the letter the minimum dimensions of 3,000 feet by 300 feet of the airstrip. It also needed to be as smooth and level as we could make it. Don had left Ethiopian money in a locked box. He wanted me to hire as many Anuaks as I could use and pay them $3 Ethiopian a day. He believed there would be enough money to get the work done. From time to time, at least once a month or every two weeks if possible, a runner would come from the mission with news, letters, and a small amount of supplies such as medicine. If we needed something urgently between those times, I was to send a runner, and they would be paid for the trip at the mission. Our course and tasks were set for the next several months!

Thankfully, Don had planned the building of the new mission on the Gilo River to begin at the start of the dry season. We were fortunate he did this. The dry season started in September and ended in the spring, and when the dry season starts, it does not rain at all. We didn't have to worry about getting wet or trying to work in muddy conditions. But once the dry season ends, it ends completely. I was there when it ended. There had been no rain for months, then one day, clouds came over and it rained hard. It rained at least once every day after that.

CHAPTER SEVEN

MALARIA:
"IT MUST BE THE INSECT SPRAY"

When the letter from Don came telling us to proceed with the airstrip, I was really glad that we had already laid it out and had a good start on it. I told Omut to let the Anuaks know that I wanted to hire a group of them to clear the airstrip and to tell them that anyone wanting to work should be at the camp early tomorrow. The next day, even before we had finished our breakfast, there were Anuaks waiting. I had Omut come with me to translate. I told them what I wanted them to do and that I had been authorized to pay them $3 Ethiopian each day. We would start work about this time each day and quit before sundown with a break for lunch, but we could not provide lunch. I also told them they would be paid on Saturday and no work on Sunday. I asked Omut to make sure they understood, and he said they did. When I asked how many wanted to work, all but just a few raised their hands. I told those who did not want to work to leave. Then I began grouping those who stayed into groups with at least one big, strong-looking guy in each group. I ended up with six groups of four each. I asked Omut if there would be any problem if I grouped the men like this, and he didn't think so, so I handed out the tools. Dave, Chuck, and I would also work, but we'd also have to supervise the Anuaks' work.

Through Omut I told the men that we would continue working in the same way we had begun. They would clear the brush and small trees, next the trees, then the termite hills, and then chop out the stumps. I would mark the edges of the airstrip each day before work began by chopping blazes in trees or just cutting small trees.

The work was a little chaotic at first, but fairly soon we seemed to be getting into a routine. It was evident right away that Chuck, Dave, and I would not get much work done ourselves as we had to keep going from group to group to keep everyone on task. We would tell them to clear an area or cut a tree and, when that was done, to go on to the next thing. They never would. They would just stop and wait for us to tell them what to do. The first day Chuck, Dave, and I were exhausted, not from physical labor, but from trying to keep the Anuaks working.

The next day was a little better, but we noticed even when they had not finished a task, some of them were just standing around. I thought maybe they were tired and not used to hard work, but they didn't look that tired. When I asked Omut about it, he told me, "No, they aren't tired, just lazy! They drink too much beer at night." The work slowed down even more when a strip had been cleared and everyone was needed to level the area. This was hard, boring work. We made it through Friday and I decided we all needed a two-day rest. So I paid the men and told them we would start again early Monday. We appreciated the break. Dave, Chuck, and I spent the two days relaxing, doing some reading, writing letters for the next runner, hand washing clothes, and recuperating. We decided we needed to talk about the work and see if we could figure out how to make it more productive and not so time consuming with us supervising. All we could come up with was that we needed a way to motivate them to work without constant supervision, and we didn't have any creative ideas about how to do that.

Monday morning we got up and had breakfast as usual. I noticed that when the men were gathering, there were two groups. There was a smaller group somewhat apart from the other larger group. I also noticed that in the smaller group there were men we did not have to constantly supervise. In fact, some of them were the ones who had volunteered to help even before we offered to pay for the work.

When it came time to give out the tools, only a few men came forward. I asked Omut to find out what was going on. After a few minutes he came back and told me, "The men over there want more money." At first I was upset and worried that we couldn't get the job done without them, and I did not believe that we had enough money to pay more. Then my mind calmed completely as I had the thought, *I do not have to worry. This is all in God's hands and God will work it out if we just trust and follow our hearts.* I told Omut that there wasn't any more money to pay them and to tell them that anyone wanting to continue as agreed could come get their tools. I watched him telling the others and also saw that they tried arguing with Omut, but he would have none of it. All at once, they stormed off. Omut came back and said they would not work unless I paid them more, as I had lots of money and was just being a selfish, rich American.

At first, I just laughed as I thought of our torn, dirty clothes, ragged shoes, and our tents and cots. Then I thought, *Well, compared to what they have, I guess we are rich.* I told Omut thank you and to thank those men when he saw them for reminding me just how well off we were. I went over to where the smaller group of Anuaks was waiting. There were just eight of them. I handed them all tools and Chuck, Dave, and I got tools as well. We divided in three groups with either me, Dave, or Chuck in a group and went to work. We took our usual lunch break and decided to share some of our lunch with the eight men also. As we looked at what we had accomplished that morning, it seemed that we had made good progress and it was clear that we were much more relaxed; we even laughed at times. By the end of that first day after my first (and last) labor strike, it was clear that with only eight men and us working, we were getting at least as much done as we had with twenty-four Anuaks. In this case, as is true in many situations, less was definitely more.

The next morning we decided we would like to start each day with a brief morning prayer. I asked Omut to ask the other Anuaks if that would be all right with them. They were all okay with the idea. I also asked Omut to pray out loud with us in Anuak and invite any of them who wanted to, to do the same. From that day forward we started each workday with a brief prayer group. Omut and I always said a brief prayer, sometimes Chuck or Dave would say a prayer, and every once in a while, one or two of the Anuaks would pray as well. After about three weeks, a group of ten Anuaks showed up to start the morning work. I recognized some of them as being part of the group that wanted more money. I asked Omut to find out what they wanted. After talking with them briefly he came back and said they wanted to work. I told Omut to tell them politely that I was glad they were willing to work, but at this time I did not have need of any more workers. When he went back to tell them I could see they were disappointed, but it seemed to me they did not seem to be surprised. It seemed to me they did not really expect to be hired. I went over to where they were and thanked them again and had Omut tell them that there might be additional work in the future. I also asked Omut to record their names so that if we did need workers they would be the first ones we asked. I could see this made them feel much better.

As I mentioned, cobras loved termite hills. We left the termite hills for last as we cleared so that it would be completely clear around the hills before we attacked them. We always had three men working on a hill. One would chop into the hill and the other two would watch, ready to kill the cobras when they came out. Not every hill had cobras, but we killed several every week. During the eight months we worked on the airstrip and

The cobra not only has very powerful venom in a bite, it can spit the stuff quite accurately into your eyes!

other projects, we never had a single accident of a serious nature, nor did anyone get bitten by the cobras. That is a very unusual record for a group using dangerous axes, picks, and mattocks. It is clear that we received special protection during this time.

We continued with our small group of workers through the completion of the airstrip with no more labor problems. We found we were getting more work done and actually enjoying it. We also had the pleasure of working side by side with the Anuaks. They came to be our friends and colleagues. They now felt free to suggest doing things a little differently, and it usually worked better. It seemed to me that once more God had shown us the better way.

The excitement and newness of the adventure that had been thrust upon us began to wear off after a few weeks. We had settled into a daily repetitive routine. It was then that our isolation began to hit us. Chuck's best friend, Charlie, was not with him. They had planned the trip with Dr. McClure as a joint adventure, and now they were forced to be apart. Chuck and Charlie had grown up together. They went to the same schools and attended the same church in a suburb of Pittsburgh. The separation was especially difficult for Chuck.

One evening after supper, Chuck said, "I have to go back to Pokwo. I need to see how Charlie is doing." Dave and I were pretty shocked by this statement. Neither of us was aware of how much Chuck missed Charlie, probably because both of us were trying to deal with how lonely we were getting. Fortunately, we kept our cool and did not say what was surely on both our minds: "What do you mean you're leaving us to go back to Pokwo? How could you even think of such a thing? You can't leave us here and go back." After we had gotten over the shock a little, we said, "Well let's discuss this together. In order for you to return, you'll need a guide. It's at least sixty miles on animal trails and none of us has the least idea how to get there. The only Anuak who speaks any English is Omot, our cook, and we have to have him here to help us. We can't all go and leave all of Dr. McClure's belongings here; they would all disappear before we even got to Pokwo."

I said, "Chuck, as important as those obstacles are, there is another far more important issue. We need you here. You are a vital part of this team. Without you, I don't think we'll be able to build the airstrip. You have a really good rapport with the Anuaks, they obviously like you and work well with you. I do understand your desire to be with your best friend, Charlie. What we can do, if you wish, is send another runner back to Pokwo." Normally we waited until the messenger who came from Pokwo returned to us with another packet before sending another bunch of letters and messages. This round trip took about two weeks.

After some more discussion, Chuck said he realized it really was unreasonable for him to leave us. He said that he was just feeling so terribly lonely and homesick. Dave and I both told him that we too felt the same way. We began to realize just how hard the emotional stress was on all of us. We stayed up quite late that night just talking about what each of us were going through. As, we talked we became aware that none of us had thought of what the others were feeling, even though each of us was experiencing very similar feelings. We made a commitment to each other to be more supportive. We also made a commitment to let the others know if we began to feel overwhelmed by anything. We wanted to do what we could to prevent any of us from getting to the point of desperation again.

One evening about a week later I told Chuck and Dave that I had an insight I wanted to share with them. They knew that I tried to have a period of quiet meditation once a day. I didn't manage it all the time, but still fairly often. I told them that while I was meditating, a Bible verse came into my mind, the one in which Jesus says, "Where two or three are gathered together in my name, I am there in the midst of them."[1] I had always thought of that verse in connection with people praying together, which is also how I had heard others use it, but during my meditation it hit me that this verse need not be limited to prayer. Why not to what we were doing now? Surely if this project was something that God wanted done, then He must be right here with us. As time went on, this insight seemed to be clearly manifest. For we could not have had the success we had without God's help.

Mosquitoes were a constant problem. I had been told that after a few weeks' exposure to their bites, some people develop immunity to the itchy poison in their bites. I was pleasantly surprised to discover that I was one of the fortunate ones.

---

1. Matthew 18:20.

After a couple of weeks, I began to notice that when I was bitten, the bites did not swell as much, and then not at all, nor did I suffer any itching. This really surprised me as I had always been troubled with allergies to pollen and dust. Before we left Addis Ababa for the Gilo River, we began taking prophylactic medication to prevent malaria. The disease was endemic among all the Nilotic people. Fortunately when we first arrived at the Gilo, Don had told me where the anti-malaria medicine was kept. He also told us how much to take each day. The medicine was chloroquine phosphate (Aralin). This medication had proven to be very effective and had the fewest side effects. As soon as we realized that we boys were on our own, I took on the responsibility of making sure we all had our daily dose of Aralin each morning. We had completed our screened sleeping/eating hut and had been working on the airstrip for a while when I started feeling like I had come down with the flu. At first I continued working, but it seemed to hang on and was getting worse. I began staying in the sleeping hut and only getting out of my cot to go to the latrine and to eat something I could keep down. I also began to feel somewhat delirious at times. Finally, in a more lucid moment I realized this could not be the flu!

One of the suggested items that I brought with me to Ethiopia was *Lange's Medical Handbook.* I had referred to it a few times for various minor medical questions. As I began reading about the flu and its symptoms, I realized it did not fit what I was experiencing. I then moved on to various tropical diseases and finally malaria! I had not looked at this first because we weren't supposed to get malaria while taking the preventive medicine, but all my symptoms fit perfectly. Then I read about how to treat malaria if infected and was really pleased to see that I could use Aralin to treat the disease as well as prevent it. But then I thought, *If it isn't working to prevent it, maybe it won't work to cure it either.* I then read further and read about the correct dosage for preventing malaria. BINGO! We had been taking half the recommended dosage of Aralin. At first I thought I had made a mistake, but when I went to the cabinet where we kept it, there was the note Don wrote specifying how much we should take. It said just half the amount we should take! Then I realized that when Don wrote this, he also was ill and that must have caused him to make the mistake.

I immediately got the other fellows together and told them what had happened and that I believed I had malaria. I had them take the correct dose and told them to watch carefully for the beginning symptoms. I began taking the large doses required to treat the disease. I felt huge relief just from having a good idea of what was going on with me, as well as something positive to do about it. I still did not feel well so I stayed in the sleeping hut most of the time. *Lange's* said it could take as long as a week or more to really feel better. I did feel well enough at times to read even though I was very weak.

We had quite a few books, though, until then, I had not had time to read any. When I read for a while, I would often find myself falling asleep. One day, dozing on my cot after reading, I heard a strange sound. It sounded like a can of insect spray had fallen over and was spraying under my cot. We only used the spray in our hut to kill any mosquitoes that got in. We were trying to make it last as long as possible. So my first thought was, "Oh no, I'm wasting our spray!" I was just ready to reach under the cot to grab the spray can when something stopped me. How could a can of spray just start spraying by itself? It didn't sound just right either. I carefully peered over the side of my cot and saw not a can of spray but a very large snake. I was able to work my way down to the other end of the cot and not disturb the snake. I got a stick I had been using as a cane to help me walk to the latrine and held the snake down while calling for help. An Anuak came and dispatched the snake with his spear.

It was not a cobra but a spreading viper, a snake whose bite causes a wound that will not heal and often requires the amputation of the affected limb. Once more my angel had protected me, first by helping find a cure for malaria and then from the probable bite of the snake, had I followed my first impulse to reach under the cot. I realized what a close call I had had. I gave very grateful thanks to the One who is All Ways (always) present.

The Nile crocodile is not something you want to be in the water with, nor even near on land.

CHAPTER EIGHT

A CROCODILE THREATENS
OUR NEIGHBORS

The Gilo River where we were camped is home to the infamous Nile crocodile. We saw them swimming in the river once in a while. We also had been warned to watch carefully for crocs when we went to bathe, especially if we went for a swim. Sometimes crocs would lie in wait under water and watch for someone to come down to get a bucket of water. Crocs can move unbelievably fast. We were to always have two people watching, one upstream and one downstream, if we were brave (foolish) enough to go swimming in the river.

There was an Anuak village just a little way up river from our camp. The river took a sharp bend right where the airstrip began. Around that bend and up a little way was the Anuak village. It was across the river from our campsite. We could easily hear the drums and singing when they had a dance to celebrate something. One day some men came running into our camp shouting. Since none of our group understood their language, I asked Omut what was going on. I could see that the men were very upset. They kept yelling and pointing up the river toward their village. After a few minutes, Omut came to me and told me what had happened. There was a very big crocodile that stayed not far from that village. The Anuaks saw it sunning itself on a sandbar almost daily just a little way down river from their village. The Anuaks tried to be very careful about watching for this croc when they went down to the water's edge for any reason. Crocs were known to grab grown men and women at the edge of the river when they came to wash their hands and faces or to get a pot of water. On this day, a child had been playing in the shallow water near their village where the women were washing clothes. For some reason, no one noticed that the child had wandered a little farther downstream than the women. Their method of washing clothes was to rub them with plants that worked like soap, then pound them hard on rocks or logs. They had to do this several times for each piece they were washing, which created a lot of commotion. This was explained to me as the reason the women did not notice the child move away from them. The women suddenly heard the child scream, but as they looked and ran toward the child, they saw that the croc had grabbed the child and taken it underwater into the river. Of course, once the croc was gone into the river, there was nothing they could do about it. The men from the village wanted me to do something. I knew and was sure they knew that it was much too late to do anything about saving the child. They wanted me to kill the crocodile.

Dr. McClure had left his 250 Savage rifle and two boxes of shells, twenty in each box. Obviously, with so few shells, they were to be used only in an absolute emergency. I had also been told specifically not to hunt. Was this an emergency? I had Omut tell the men that I needed to think and pray about this before I could decide what, if anything, I could do. I thought and prayed about this the rest of the day. Finally, I decided that if the men spotted what they thought was the same croc, I would try to shoot it. I told Omut to have someone come tell me and to be sure not to disturb the croc. A few days passed before I heard anything. Then the men came running into camp shouting the Anuak word for croc and pointing excitedly up stream. Omut confirmed they had seen the croc. I was afraid that all the shouting and commotion may have disturbed the croc, but I got Don's rifle and some shells anyway. I tried to get the people to be quiet, but they were too excited. We were on the camp side of the river opposite the sandbar. As we neared the sandbar, they got even more excited and shouted even louder. Just as I caught view of the sandbar, I saw the croc slip into the water.

Even though the sandbar was near the village, because it was just a little around the bend in the river, it could not be seen from the village. I asked Omut to ask them what time of day they usually saw this croc. He told me it was usually early afternoon, just as it was this day. I decided that the only way I might get a shot was if I saw the croc before the Anuaks did. I decided to come to a place opposite the sandbar right after noon and wait to see if he appeared. This way I hoped to avoid having the noise from the excited Anuaks disturb the croc again. I went several days in a row and did not see the croc. I had just about decided to give it up. The next day I prayed, "God, if you want me to shoot this croc, show me." I had decided that if I went and did not see the croc, I would stop looking for it. I felt I was taking too much time away from my working on the airstrip, which was absolutely important since it was our only way to get assistance and get us and our belongings out.

I prepared carefully. I loaded the magazine with four cartridges. I had carefully cleaned and oiled the gun the night before, even though I had already done that the first time. I also tested the action to make sure it was working smoothly and the safety locked the trigger. The Savage 250 is a nice lightweight, lever action, high-powered rifle. I had never shot this model rifle. I grew up with guns and had both a deep respect and appreciation for a fine rifle. This was a very fine rifle. Before hunting with any rifle, I would normally take it to a safe place and fire at least five rounds, usually more, to see how the rifle was shooting and be certain of the point of aim. This would let me know where I had to aim to place my shot where I wanted it. In the situation I was in, however, I could not do that. First there were not any extra shells for practice, and if I were to shoot that many times, the authorities were sure to hear about it. The police were sure to use that as an excuse to take the rifle, or worse.

On one of my trips to the sandbar to watch for the croc, I had seen a tree that had an unusually shaped branch near where I needed to be to see the sandbar. It looked something like the letter J. I remembered that the Anuaks consider crocodiles Jwok, meaning something with power. I chose that branch to look for each time I came; that way I could stay back from the edge of the bank and not run the risk of being seen by the croc before I could look to see if he was there. On a previous visit when it was clear I was not going to see the croc, I had prepared a rotted log to use both as a rifle rest and to allow me to creep right up to the edge of the river with a clear view of the entire sandbar. On this day I prayed especially hard. I wanted to do what God would have me do. If that was to shoot the croc, I wanted to make a good, clean kill. I had earned the Expert Marksmanship Badge in the army for my skill in shooting. I like shooting a rifle and am good at it. My only concern was that I did not know exactly where this rifle shot when aimed.

As I walked upstream, I felt especially calm. I had prayed about it, I had prepared carefully, I was ready, and I left it in God's hands. I was even able to enjoy the beauty of the day. It was another sunny day, hot but not oppressive. I could hear birds singing, the soft lap of waves slapping the riverbank as the current turned. There was a gentle breeze blowing that helped keep me cool. It was blowing toward me so my scent would not be blown toward the croc. Even if he was there, I didn't know how keen a croc's sense of smell was. I felt it was still a good sign that my scent wasn't blowing his way. As I neared the Jwok branch, everything seemed a little different. I felt my excitement rise—this was the day! I took a few deep breaths and said a quick prayer. Most days when I neared this spot, I could hear people in the nearby village, but this day it was completely quiet.

When I got to the Jwok branch, I prepared to approach the riverbank and my log. I stopped and waited until my breath was normal and my heart had calmed. I levered a shell into the chamber, made sure the safety was on, and then began my cautious approach. I was even more careful than I had been on previous days. I crept up to my spot, keeping below the log so that the log blocked all views of the sandbar. Finally when I was almost there, I stopped and slowly raised my head. I had a tan hat that helped shield my face. As I peered over the log toward the sandbar, I saw only empty sand. My disappointment almost made me lose my cautiousness, but I kept it together, and as I looked toward the end of the sandbar upstream toward the village, I saw it! There it was, lying at the end of the sandbar and almost up against the steep bank with his nose just out of the water. The shade from the bank made him hard to see. He was faced away from me upstream toward the village, and he was huge, thirteen to fifteen feet long.

I placed the gun barrel on the log and crept slowly forward on my belly until I could raise my head and sight along the gun barrel. I maneuvered my position until I had a perfect sight picture of the croc. Once more I slowed my breathing and my heart until I felt relaxed and calm. Then I used what I had been taught: BASS, breathe, aim, sight, squeeze. This was the way to make each shot count. I aimed a little behind the croc's shoulder and a little below his back. Then I moved my aim a little further back to compensate for the angle at which he was lying.

I breathed. I aimed. I made sure my sight picture was perfect. Then I slowly squeezed the trigger. I did it so well I was startled when the gun went off. I saw the croc jump and go into the river. Did I hit him? I watched for a few minutes and then I saw blood, quite a bit of it on the water. The croc was hit and hit badly.

The Anuaks at the village heard the shot and came running, as did everyone from our camp. They were talking in Anuak and of course I didn't understand them, or they me, but they clearly understood the big grin on my face. I used the Anuak word for croc and used a cutting motion across my throat that brought smiles and a lot of laughter. When Omut got there from our camp, I told him that I had shot the croc and had seen a lot of blood. When Omut told the Anuaks from the village what I had done, they got even more excited and started pounding me on the back. They told me that if the croc was just badly injured it would stay underwater for several hours before coming up. If it was killed, it would not float to the surface for several days, so I did not know if I would ever find out for sure if I had killed the croc that had taken their child.

Three days later men from the village came to our camp and told me they had found the dead croc. Men were towing it upstream with their dugout canoes. When they got to our camp, they drug the croc out on the bank and we measured it. It was twelve and a half feet long! I examined the body to find where it was shot. I found the bullet hole perfectly placed, right where I aimed and right through the heart. God had helped me deliver a good, clean kill. I had no anger toward the croc for killing the child. The croc was just making a living, but he was making it where he endangered the Anuaks. I thanked God again for his help and then we all joined in thanksgiving to our Creator. The Anuaks knew it would be a while before another croc moved in to claim this territory, so for a while they could live a little more easily, hopefully also more carefully.

The Anuaks wanted to know if I wanted to keep the croc. I told them no, but I would like to have some of the teeth. The croc teeth are symbols of the power of the croc to the Anuaks. They told me they would be glad to bury the head and, when it was ready, remove the teeth and bring them to me. That night and for several nights we could hear the village celebrating God's gift to them. Several weeks later they brought the teeth to me as promised. I still have them.

CHAPTER NINE

WHICH WAY IS CAMP: A PILLAR OF FIRE BY NIGHT

After several weeks we had a livable camp and progress on the airstrip was proceeding well. We were getting really tired of our diet of canned tuna, Spam, and potted chicken. Only rarely did we get some fresh fish. I decided that in spite of the original message "do not hunt," we needed real meat. We were physically working very hard every day, and our bodies needed more red meat protein. I decided I would go hunting and get us some red meat. From the flight over from the Pokwo mission, I knew that there was plenty of good meat in the form of game.

When I told the Anuaks that I wanted to go hunting they got really excited. They knew that if I was successful they would have meat also, and meat was very scarce for them. I told them we would go in the afternoon, so around 2 p.m. we started out. Since I assumed the Anuaks knew the area, they led the hunt. At first I thought they were just in a hurry to get to the place they wanted to hunt. They were walking really fast, sometimes jogging. It was work to keep up. We left the main trail and took off into the bush on a faint game trail, but the Anuaks kept up the same fast pace. Every once in a while they would scare up an animal and it would burst out running away at top speed. They would shout and point, clearly expecting me to shoot. I never had a clear view of these animals, and they were always running at top speed. Even if we had been close enough for a shot, a shot at these animals at that speed would have been wasted. I would not waste a shot even if the ammunition was plentiful. I only had one box of shells. We repeated this strange (to me) exercise every day for four days.

I tried to understand why they were hunting this way. I finally realized that what they were doing fit their method of hunting very well. The Anuaks had only their spears to use for hunting; therefore, it was futile to try stealth to approach their prey. They had to rely on the animal being startled into running near someone with a spear. The Anuaks would hunt in groups. One or more groups would try to drive animals toward a group hidden in the brush or tall grass. The driving groups would attempt to scare up game and drive it toward where the others were hiding. In our case, the other half of the hunting team was missing. The group toward which an animal might be chased wasn't available. The goal was to have an animal run close enough to a man with a spear so that he could thrust his spear into the animal. Rarely was the animal killed at once. It almost always ran off. The hunters would then track the animal and hope they got to it before the large predators did. There were lions, leopards, and hyenas all eager for a free meal. This method of hunting used a tremendous amount of energy and rarely was successful. Even if they had suggested that we try that method, I wouldn't have agreed as it would be too dangerous with the rifle. Since they could not depend on hunting game for meat, the Anuaks caught fish and raised chickens and a few goats.

On the fifth day I prepared to go out again, even though I had little hope of success hunting the way we had been doing it. When I was ready to go, I did not see any of the Anuaks ready to go with me. I asked our cook, Omut, since he was the only one who could translate for me, where they were. He told me that the fellows who had been going with me weren't going today, they were too tired! I thought that was at least partially true, I knew that I was getting tired both physically and emotionally from no successful hunting. I told Omut that I would go out alone. Omut told the others and I noticed they seemed to think that was pretty amusing. I didn't think that was very nice, but given my dismal success, it was also understandable. I again left camp about 2 p.m. as usual. Since I had been out in the bush with the Anuaks, I now knew the general lay of the land. My days of going out with them had not been a total waste.

It was the time of year when the Anuaks burned the tall elephant grass. This created open areas with fresh new grass that would come up a few days after the burn. While hunting with the Anuaks I made note of several of these burn areas. I knew that the main trail ran roughly parallel with the river in a general east-west direction. I set out walking east of camp on the trail at a good fast pace for about a half hour. Then I turned and walked north for another half an hour and finally turned again heading west. I was now walking parallel to the river and to the main trail, and I knew this heading would take me toward some of those areas with fresh new grass.

This time, I hunted my way, very slowly, pausing often to scan for animals. I was also given the gift of a slight wind in my face so my scent would not blow toward the game. Believe me, I had plenty of scent! I hoped the antelope would like these burn areas as much as I did. The burn areas were usually surrounded with a fringe of brush and grass that had not burned completely. This fringe gave me a perfect place to see into the area without being seen by any animals that might be there. Each time I came near one of these fringes, I would creep forward very slowly. I was careful to make as little noise as possible and stay as low as I could until I could see through the brush and grass into the next burn area. I did this several times. I did see some antelope one time, but they were much too far away and moving away from me. Another time I saw a small group of Thomson's gazelles. They were completely unaware of me but much too small for my purposes. They are only as big as a skinny small dog. I had to wait for them to move on before I could move. I did not want to startle them and thereby alert any other game in the area.

After hunting like this for a couple of hours, I came to another fringe of brush and grass. The fringe was thin enough that I could see through it into the burn area in several places. I could see that it looked like a very nice burn area with lots of new grass a few inches tall. I approached this fringe very carefully and slowly. Since I could see through it, I knew any animals that might be there could also see me, and their eyesight was probably far superior to mine. The clothing I wore helped me also. I was quite well camouflaged, not as originally designed, but because of the daily work in the dirt and no laundry facilities other than the river water, my clothes were about the same color as my surroundings. They had plenty of stains on them and had become somewhat ragged. I was also dirty and well-tanned. I blended quite well with the mostly brown and tan landscape.

As I approached, I picked a spot with plenty of cover where I could get near with less risk of being seen if there were any animals there. I slowly crept through the cover until I could see into the burn area. Then I stopped and began scanning. At first I didn't see anything. Then, almost in the shade on the other side, I saw something big. I couldn't see it clearly so I didn't know what it was, but I knew it was big. As I watched, not moving a muscle and scarcely breathing, I saw this big waterbuck move out into the open grazing on the new grass. This was a big animal about the size of a bull elk. It was a long shot but well within the range of Don's rifle. The rifle was a Savage 250 Model 99 lever action with iron sights. It shot the 250–3000 cartridge, which was the first American commercial cartridge to achieve 3,000 feet per minute muzzle velocity and shot a .25 caliber 87 grain bullet. This is a very flat shooting rifle. I would have to be very careful with only iron sights to place my shot just right. The bullet was small for this size animal, but if done right, it could do the job. The waterbuck was moving slowing as he grazed and angled toward me. It did not make for a good shot. I knelt, watched, and waited as the animal grazed. The good news was he was slowly moving toward me, not away. The shot would be a little shorter. As I waited, the animal began to slowly turn as he grazed, until he was in a perfect broadside position.

Because of the grass and brush, to get a clear shot I would have to kneel to shoot. The rifle had a sling that I could use to help stabilize the rifle for the shot. I had been trained to use a sling for shooting in the army. When I got into position, I rested and calmed myself. I prayed, "God, if it is good and right for me to kill this beautiful creature of your creation, please help me to make a clean kill. If you don't want me to take this beautiful creature, please make sure I miss completely so that I do not injure him."

I now had a good sight picture. The waterbuck was standing so his side was toward me and not moving. I used BASS: breathe, aim, sight, squeeze. I judged the animal to be about 150 yards away, a long shot with iron sights but a possible shot if I did everything just right. I knew the Savage 250 was a flat shooting rifle. What I didn't know was for what range Don had sighted the rifle. Would he have sighted in at seventy-five yards so the rifle bullet would hit exactly where aimed at seventy-five yards? That would be a conservative and a fairly easy distance to shoot. Or, because this was mostly open country, did he choose one hundred yards for the point of aim? I didn't know and was unable to check due to limited shells and the risk of test shots being reported to the police. I couldn't risk losing Don's rifle.

So I did the only thing I could: I prayed, and then I had the feeling that Don had probably chosen one hundred yards. This meant that if the waterbuck was 150 yards away as I guessed, I needed to aim about two to three inches higher than where I wanted the bullet to hit. I aimed behind the front shoulder and a little higher than the point of the shoulder, compensating for the bullet drop, and raised my sights a couple of inches. Breathe, aim, sight, and squeeze. I gently squeezed the trigger. The rifle bucked, but only after the shot. The waterbuck jerked but did not move. I thought I had missed him and was about to take another shot when he fell over and did not move. I quickly ran to it with my rifle ready for another shot if he got up. He never moved a muscle. I was both pleased and surprised to see it had been a perfect shot and a clean kill.

This picture is nearly identical to the view I had when shooting the waterbuck. I don't know how it could have been better.

I paused to thank God and got to work. The animal was so big there was no way I could field dress him. I needed help and a lot of it. It was almost sundown and I knew I was at least two hours from camp. It would be dark when I got back to camp and even darker when we returned. There was no moon at that time. I decided I would cut off the hind quarters and at least get them back safely. I was worried that predators and scavengers would get to the animal before we got back. I quickly cut off the hind quarters and then tied them together at the hock with strips of hide I cut from the water buck so that I could put them over my shoulder to carry. They were very heavy, probably close to one hundred pounds. I draped them over my shoulder, turned, and headed as nearly directly south as I could judge from the sun. I walked a short distance and then I turned around to see if there was anything I could use to help guide us back to this spot. There near the waterbuck was one tall tree with only a few branches. Then I needed something to line the tree up with. There on the horizon was the glow of a grass burn, directly in line with the tree. I turned toward the trail and walked as fast as I could with my heavy load. I paused from time to time and looked back to be sure I was still walking in line with the tree and the glow of the fire. Finally I hit the main trail. I looked at my watch. It had taken me a half hour to walk from the kill to the trail. I found a branch I could hang the legs from and then I dragged a big branch across the trail to mark the spot. It was now getting pretty dark. I started jogging toward camp.

I was exhausted when I got back to camp. The camp

was in an uproar worried about what had happened to me. Had I fallen and injured myself, had an accident with the rifle, or had one of the large predators attacked me? Since they didn't know where I went, they didn't even know where to look for me. When I came into camp they thought I was badly hurt because I was covered in blood! First I had to convince them that I was fine, just exhausted, and then that I had killed a big waterbuck. They couldn't believe it, but all the blood helped convince them. I told them I had marked the location and needed them to come quickly to get the meat before other animals got to it. Chuck came with me and we both brought our flashlights. Omut and six other Anuaks came along. I hurried down the trail. It seemed much shorter going back and I was a little surprised how soon we came to the branch across the trail. There were the hindquarters of the waterbuck I had killed. I think it was only then that they believed me. One of the Anuaks took the two hindquarters and headed back to camp with them.

I turned toward the north and there was the glow on the horizon. I checked my watch and headed toward the glow. While returning for the waterbuck and following the beacon of fire on the distant horizon, I was vividly reminded of the Biblical story in Exodus 13:21: "And the Lord went before them to show the way by day in a pillar of a cloud, and by night in a pillar of fire: that he might be the guide of their journey at both times." I had not consciously thought about that story of how Yahweh guided the Israelites' journey in the wilderness. When the story came into my mind, I thought, "Well how appropriate. In the Biblical story God was providing for the children of Israel not only food but also a guide for their way through the wilderness, and here He is guiding us to the meat I sincerely believed God provided."

After a half hour I stopped and looked around. It didn't look that familiar and there was no dead animal or sign of one. We searched for a little bit with no luck. I kept looking for that tall tree with few limbs. I stopped to think what might be the problem. Then it hit me. The fire would be moving. While hunting, I had been walking into the wind. It was only a slight breeze. That meant the fire would have been moving to our right as we faced it. I turned to the west and started walking. After only a short distance, I saw the tall tree with few branches. Shortly after that I saw my waterbuck, still there and not damaged by scavengers. Again I thanked God for guidance and protection. I was reminded of the "pillar of fire by night" that God used for Moses and wondered if it was something like my glow on the horizon. The Anuaks were beside themselves with joy. There would be plenty of meat for them, their families, and us. They immediately began to butcher the waterbuck, and in a short time they had all the edible pieces wrapped in pieces of skin to carry back.

When they were nearly done, I asked Omut, "Which way is camp?" He looked sort of puzzled, and then he began talking with the other Anuaks. They talked for some time. Every once in a while one of them would point one way. They would talk some more and another would point in a completely different direction. Sometimes I saw two of them at once pointing in opposite directions. This was not good! I had expected such a simple question would have gotten a response like one of the Anuaks pointing toward camp saying, "That way." It suddenly hit me that they did not know which way camp was. I was stunned. I then realized that the Anuaks do not go anywhere at night. It isn't safe. They had not learned to use the stars to guide them. I decided even though it would be a longer walk than heading directly toward camp, we could be more certain of where to go by going back the way we came. We headed as directly south as I could determine using the North Star to guide me. We came to the main trail near where we had left it and I had hung the hind quarters. I was really exhausted by this time. I was also exhilarated by the success of the hunt and even more by being able to find the animal and bring all the meat back.

The next day in camp and in the nearby village, there was much celebration. Every bit of the waterbuck would be used. We built a screened cage that we hung in a tree and then put wet towels over it to keep the meat cool and free from flies. We were able to keep some of the meat for a week. God is good indeed!

This Anuak man from Gambela is named Omot Ochan. His appearance is remarkably similar to our cook, our translator, our friend, Omot. He very well could be a near relative of our cook.

CHAPTER TEN

THANKSGIVING ON THE GILO: A STRANGE DESSERT

One of the important pieces of luggage that Dr. McClure brought with him on his return to Ethiopia from the States was several foot lockers filled with donated sample medications. These had been given to him by medical people to use to help the people he served. Several times while we were working on the airstrip, Anuaks had come asking for medicine for various problems. The people knew it was Don's practice to give out medicine when he was at the station. I had been instructed not to do that even if I thought I knew what might help. Nothing serious came to our camp, so I did not feel too badly about turning them away.

One day a woman came in with a terrible burn on the top of her head. I said I could not help her and turned her away. I felt really badly about it and very conflicted. She came back a few days later and I could see the burn was very infected and could only get worse. I decided I had to do something; I could not ignore her suffering. So, with Omut's help, I cleaned the wound as best I could, put topical antibiotic on it, and bandaged the wound. The burn was so bad and had become so infected, I did not see how it could heal. I told her to come back each day and I would dress the wound.

When I asked what had happened, I learned that this woman had a bad problem with the homemade beer the Anuaks make. It was usually used only at special celebrations. She had gotten some and kept it for herself. She drank it, got drunk, and fell where her head got in the fire. She kept coming back each day for the wound to be dressed. After a couple of days, I could see that the wound had begun to heal. After a week it had healed enough that I felt she could care for it herself, so I gave her a small tube of antibiotic and told her, through Omut, how to dress it and clean it.

I did not see her after that. One day a smiling woman came into camp with a young girl carrying a basket of tomatoes. Omut said they wanted to give me the tomatoes. When he saw that I did not know who they were, he told me she was the woman whose head I had helped to dress and her daughter. The woman then took off her headscarf and showed me the wound had completely healed. Once more I gave thanks for the amazing way God works. The tomatoes were a very special gift as they do not raise many of them, and they know how much Americans like tomatoes. We had not had any fresh vegetables since our arrival.

* * *

We had been working hard and progress was going along well on the airstrip, but we needed encouragement. As usual what you really need, as opposed to what you think you need, is always met, often in ways least expected. Our messenger from Pokwo had been as regular as possible. He usually arrived either on Saturday or Sunday, every other week. We counted on his arrival because he always brought us mail, and he usually brought a surprise treat of some kind. One time it was chocolate candy (a little soft but tasted great), and another time he brought in fresh eggs. That was a real surprise because they are so fragile. He was due to arrive and we were eager for him. He usually got there by noon, which was fast approaching.

On the days we expected the messenger, we quit work early; today was no exception. We had been sitting in the shade talking about what mail we might get and from whom we really wanted to hear. We heard shouting in Anuak down the trail and then an American voice. "Hello, Chuck and Daves!" We ran to the head of the trail and there was Charlie. His leg had finally healed enough for him to make the five-day hike overland through the bush. That was the best surprise and gift we could have imagined. It also convinced me to go ahead with something I had been thinking about but had not told the other fellows. Now, with all of us together it seemed very appropriate. I felt we needed a special celebration.

I had been thinking about giving thanks for another reason. Often at the end of the day, or just before falling asleep at night, I would review in my mind the day's events. I would think about what we had accomplished, and how we were able to do all these things. Where did that knowledge and skill come from? I realized as I reflected on the information and skills that I used daily, they all were gifts from my parents. I learned a deep faith in God from each of them. Mother was very vocal about her faith, but Dad simply lived it. I am the youngest of four boys. We were all taught to be self-reliant, not in words but in daily life. We were also taught to depend on each other and how to care for all the family. Even though my brothers were sometimes quite a pain, and I am sure I was also, we knew we could depend on each other. Having no sisters, we all learned how to cook, how to clean house, how to do the laundry, how to iron the clothes, and even how to sew. No one picked up after us.

We learned to be responsible for ourselves, our home, and our animals, and shared responsibility for the whole family. We raised most of our own food. I learned how to prepare foods for storage, how to can, how to preserve meat, and even how to render lard and make soap. From Dad I learned how to take whatever was available and build what was needed with the tools at hand. I learned how to care for our animals and the land. I learned how to raise all our own vegetables. I also learned how to hunt, fish, and prepare the game or fish that were gotten. Most importantly I learned to be satisfied and grateful for what God had given us. No time or energy was wasted on wishing things were different. As I reflected on our lives there in the midst of "primitive" Africa, I really appreciated what a wonderful preparation I had been given for this experience. That evening I wrote to my parents to tell them how grateful I was for all they had given me, and how important those gifts were to me in our daily lives.

Thanksgiving was near. I thought that it would be great if we could put together something close to a traditional Thanksgiving dinner. I had talked with Omot about this and he was pleased to do something special for us. He said we had canned sweet potatoes and canned green beans, and he could make a dressing with cornmeal; also, he could make gravy if I could get the "bird." There actually is a large bird that some Americans use as a substitute for turkey. It's called a bustard, but I had never seen one and the Anuaks didn't know what it was either. I think they were unfamiliar with the name. I had not seen a large bird other than emperor storks, so we would have to improvise. There were quite a lot of guinea fowl around; however, their meat is quite dark and a little gamey. Finally I decided to see if I could get some of the numerous doves, which are similar to our turtle doves only more the size of pigeons. Yes, I know, that is a very small turkey!

There was a water hole not too far from camp where I had seen doves. That is where I decided to go to get Thanksgiving dinner. I knew that I would have to shoot them no earlier than the day before our meal, as it would be hard to keep them fresh. I went to the water hole each day for several days to see when the best time would be. The doves were there early in the morning but very restless, so I would have to get there really early. I found that they came to the water hole late in afternoon to drink and bathe after feeding during the day, and they were not as restless. I guess a full tummy made them content. The day before Thanksgiving, I got the shotgun, some shells, and a water bottle for me and headed to the water hole so I would be there before the doves came back. When I got to the water hole I looked for a place where I could conceal myself but have both a clear view and an open shot at the birds. When I found what I thought was a good spot, I settled myself. I then prayed to God asking that if it was good for us to have these doves that He would help me have good, clean kills, or if it wasn't the thing for me to do that I would miss completely. That would be easy because I did not consider myself a particularly good bird shooter with a shotgun. Even though I grew up hunting pheasants and quail on our farm, I was never very good at it.

Sure enough, late afternoon I heard the first bunch coming in. They landed by the water's edge and began drinking and preening. I stood up and was able to get two before the others flew. After picking up the two fallen doves, I sat back down in my mostly concealed spot and waited. Fortunately these doves had not been hunted, so even though the explosion of the shots certainly frightened them, when they could see no obvious danger they returned. Just as this first bunch returned, another larger group came flying in. There was much milling about and strutting as well as drinking and bathing. I let them settle a little before standing and again was able to get off two clean shots and two more doves. When the doves returned, they were more skittish and I got too anxious. I tried to get a shot at one while they were still coming in and missed completely. That time I had to wait quite awhile before I heard birds coming in. I had learned my lesson. I waited until they came in, settled down, and were pretty calm. I was again able to get two more doves. I decided that was enough for a small Thanksgiving dinner. We could always supplement the doves with some Spam.

When I brought the doves back to camp the other three were pretty surprised. "What are those for?" they asked. I had not told the others about my plan because I wanted it to be a surprise. They all laughed when I told them the doves were our Thanksgiving turkey. Then I told them about the rest of the planned dinner. They had forgotten it was Thanksgiving, or at least hadn't said anything about it. I had asked Omot to tell the Anuak workers that we were taking that day off. The next morning we were up as usual. It is pretty hard to sleep with the sun shining in your eyes, especially when we went to bed as soon as it was dark. Omot had made us pancakes for breakfast as a special treat for our day. We tried to stay out of Omot's way, but I think he got tired of us asking if we could help. We finally decided that we would use the time until dinner by taking baths in the river, washing our clothes, and cleaning up our living area in the screen house. This turned out to be a good plan, as it kept us busy and from pestering Omot.

We were still working in the screen house when Omot

came to the door and announced that our dinner was ready. We usually ate outside under a tree and had a table with benches set up for that purpose. When we came out to the table we all had a surprise. The table was nicely set up with a tablecloth and cloth napkins. Omot had found them in our stored goods. Apparently Lyda had packed these in the early shipments. In the center of the table was a glass jar with wild lilies. It was perfect. Before we sat down, I asked Omot to join us. We all held hands and gave thanks for all the wonderful gifts God had given us, including this wonderful surprise. We were to have one more surprise for our Thanksgiving dinner that would give us all a good laugh. Omot brought each dish to the table and served each of us. The menu was as planned: green beans with dried onions, brown sugar glazed sweet potatoes, fresh baked rolls, stuffed roasted doves, cornmeal dressing, and gravy. It was delicious. No five-star restaurant could have equaled the quality of care and love that went into this meal and surrounded us in our company. True the doves only gave us a few bites, but it was still our special Thanksgiving dinner.

Then Omot brought out the surprise, pumpkin pie! Even I did not know he planned to do this. He served each of us and we each took a bite. What a surprise—it was pumpkin pie all right, but a little something was missing. It is important to realize that Omot cooked strictly from memory. He had forgotten a rather crucial ingredient, the sugar! We all had a good laugh. After Omot got over his embarrassment, he too was able to laugh at the mistake. We assured him that even though the pie didn't quite do what he intended, the fact that he went to all the special effort for our meal was truly a gift of love. We told Omot that he could not clean up as he usually did. We wanted to do this much for him. Finally he accepted our offer after we insisted that we really wanted to do it. Our Thanksgiving was a huge success. God had truly blessed us again.

CHAPTER ELEVEN

FIRST AIRPLANE INTO THE GILO: EIGHT MONTHS OF HARD WORK COMPLETED

The work on the airstrip was always our primary task, and its completion was our number one goal. The initial plan turned out to be the most effective: remove the brush and small trees, cut down the big trees, chop down termite hills, remove tree stumps, and level the cleared area. Sometimes, I think because we got bored doing the same thing, we would try doing things differently; for example, we'd just start clearing everything and work across a new strip of the airstrip. These attempts at doing it differently always turned out to have problems, usually in the form of getting in each other's way, so we always returned to that first plan.

God really did know what he was doing. There were a couple of things we did add to the clearing plan that were useful and added a little variety. After we had only a couple of completely cleared strips, we realized we had a lot of debris gathering on the edge of the airstrip. This did not seem like a good idea.

We decided that the brush and very small trees would be put in piles in the cleared area to burn when it was dry. Where we had an area of the tall elephant grass, we would cut it and tie it in a bundle with strands of grass. We carried this to an area near the camp to store for use as roofing thatch. The big trees usually had some fairly long, straight sections. We would trim these and take them to a storing location near the camp. These would be used when Don started building additional buildings for the new mission. We even saved branches that could be used as roof supports for the grass thatch or for other purposes. All this took a little extra time, but we felt it was worth it as it would save time later and not waste useful resources.

One day in the afternoon as we were all working on the airstrip, an Anuak not working with us came running and shouting while he pointed down river. We looked down river and saw smoke. Someone had started a fire, perhaps to burn the tall grass, but they were usually very careful to not do this near their villages. We all ran with our tools and began trying to create a firebreak, a cleared area so the fire could not get to our camp. The grass we had gathered and stored was on the side of camp near the fire. We all worked as hard as we could, and we were having success protecting most of the camp. It became evident we could not save the stored grass. Some of us began moving the grass bundles stored nearest to our camp by just throwing them farther away.

The Anuak village people had come to help and brought pots, pans, anything to hold water, and brought con-

tainers of water to the side of our camp closest to the fire. Sometimes a spark would fly into the camp area and it would be
quickly quenched with the water. People began bringing containers and throwing water on the roof of the screen house to
make it less flammable. When we realized we needed to do
more, we took some of the bundles of grass and laid them in a
row, and then started a backfire toward the approaching fire.
Everyone worked as hard as possible. Finally just before the
blaze got to our fire, the wind shifted slightly and drove the fire
parallel to camp rather than straight toward us. I looked up and
saw the whole stack of stored grass blazing in a huge fire. This
big fire was actually creating its own wind, sucking air toward
it. This had the effect of pulling, not only the wild fire, but also
our backfire toward it. Our stack of stored grass had saved the
camp and all our things. God does work in mysterious ways to
perform His wonders! We all kept vigil and watched for sparks.
We used the containers of water to quench any stray sparks. It
took a couple of hours before the fire died down to a level that
we could relax a little. When it looked safe enough, we all had
a thanksgiving prayer group.

We never did learn who started the grass fire or why.
It seemed pretty suspicious. The local Anuaks from the village
were very upset. It seemed that they were afraid someone from
their village had started the fire, either stupidly or intentionally.
Either way, they were afraid the whole village would be blamed.
It was a couple of days before Omot told me about the village people's concern. Apparently they had been so afraid they

didn't even want Omot to know. One of our workers finally told him. I had Omot get our workers together and talked with them about this. I wanted to make clear that in no case would I blame the whole village, even if one of them started the fire. I also wanted to thank the people from the village for their help in protecting our camp.

They told me that the village king was the one to go to. They called the head man in the village, king. He is always one of the oldest males and is believed to have extra power, somewhat like a shaman. He is also considered to be Jwok. They said if I could think of a way to honor him, the entire village would take this as an honor as well. I thought about this and asked Omot if giving him the horns from the waterbuck would be considered appropriate. The Anuaks cut off the horns and I kept them, even though I knew I would not be able to take them back to the States with me. Omot said he was sure the king and the whole village would be honored. So I then asked Omot if he could arrange it. He told me he would talk with our workers. One of them had special stature in the village. He was bigger and stronger than the others. He always wore a large ivory band on his upper arm. Omot brought this man to me and we talked. He said we should let the king know we wanted to honor the village and the king, and we wanted it to be a special occasion. I said I did not think I should do that as I was not the "chief," Dr. McClure was, and he wasn't here. I asked this elder if he would explain this to the king and present the waterbuck horns to him for Dr. McClure and us. He thought about it and decided that would be okay, especially since Dr. McClure could not do it and I should not try to take his place. That would be considered trying to "steal power." I assured him I did not want to do that but did want to show respect and our thankfulness for the village's help. I also wanted them to be reassured that we did not blame them for the fire.

The elder took the horns and I did not hear anything for several days. Then, one day I heard a commotion. Some Anuak men were coming down the trail. They all had old jackets on. Their hair was made up in the style they use only for special occasions. These hairdos are quite interesting. They use cow dung and ashes mixed into a paste-like mixture, and then mold their hair into very unique shapes. When it dries, it will stay that way for quite a while. So they don't break the hairdo when they sleep, they use a wooden pillow to prop their heads up and keep the hairdo off the ground. Some of these pillows are just pieces of small branches with side branches like legs. Others are elaborately carved from a piece of wood.

Two or three of these men carried old rifles. In the middle of this group of men was an old man who walked with a cane. He had long gray hair. He wore many necklaces of bone, metal, and wood. I thought I saw one that had some gold in it. He also wore a long military overcoat with some of the campaign ribbons still on it. It looked like my father's World War I army coat. When the Anuak men in our camp saw this, they all moved away. Omot came over to me and whispered, "This is the king from the village!" I asked what I should do. Omot said he would get chairs for us. I started to get one myself and Omot stopped me and said, "No, you wait with him until I bring a chair to you." Then I understood this was to be a very special occasion. If I got the chair myself, it would show disrespect for him and lower my status before him. Saving face is everything!

I waited and no one spoke. Omot first brought a chair to me and waited until I sat. Then he brought a chair for the king and placed him in front of me about six feet away. Once the king sat, his cadre of men sat on the ground. Some sat to the side and some sat behind but none in front of the king. Omot also sat near me to the side. I gestured for Dave, Chuck, and Charlie to come sit beside me and they did. As soon as we were all seated, the king began to speak. After he spoke for a little while, I held up my hand for him to stop. I asked Omot to explain that I wanted to hear and understand the king and we would ask Omot to translate for us. When Omot told the king what I wanted, he nodded. He began to speak again in short speeches, waiting for Omot to translate each time. The gist of what he said was that he had come to thank me for the great honor I had given him with the waterbuck horns. He also wanted me to know that his village welcomed us as neighbors. One of the men brought forward a goatskin. In it was the set of waterbuck horns I had given him. He began to speak again and held out the set of horns toward me. At first I thought he was giving them back to me. Omot translated and told me the king would like me to bless the horns since I was the one to whom the waterbuck had given his life.

I was really moved by this whole event. I realized here was an opportunity to give thanks to God with these new neighbors. I took the horns. Then I thanked the king for honoring us in this way. I said I was sorry that our king, Dr. Don McClure, could not be here to properly receive this honor. I was glad to do this in his place. I then raised the horns and first I thanked the waterbuck for giving his life that we and our neighbors might have the gift of his meat. I thanked God for the waterbuck as a gift of his creation and then thanked God for bringing us all together as one village with our Father God as our King. When I finished I handed the horns back to the king. He seemed to be pleased. I thought once more if we just trust God to guide us, amazing and wonderful things happen. It seemed clear that God had used this affair—the fire, the villagers helping us, their worry, and finally this exchange of gifts and honors—to help build a bridge, even a bond, between the new mission and the Anuak village.

* * *

We had cleared all trees, termite hills, and removed all tree stumps, but the airstrip was far from finished. A pilot could have certainly used the field for an emergency landing but would never be able to take off. It was far too rough. Usually at this point, a truck or tractor would start dragging a heavy drag over the ground to smooth it out. I knew we would need to do this, so I had been thinking about an idea that would work. We had lots of big logs and smaller ones as well. We made a drag out of one log about ten inches in diameter and another smaller one about six inches in diameter. The small log would be the front drag and the bigger log the back. I connected these two with several small logs. We then attached some heavy ropes to it to see if we could drag it. It took three men where the ground was really rough, but after it got smoother, two men would do. Dragging at an angle pushed dirt to one side or the other. It worked rather well. It was very hard work, so two men could not do it for long. Two or three men would pull on the first pass, and then two more had shovels to fill in low spots and break up clumps of dirt. Occasionally they would discover part of a root sticking out that we missed and have to chop it out. They also found lots of short pieces of wood that had to be cleared so they wouldn't be picked up by airplane propellers.

While the airstrip was being leveled and smoothed, I took the other men with me. First we went to the end by the river and removed all trees and brush over six feet high. This was so airplanes could come in low over the river and land right at the end of the runway. Removing these obstacles would allow planes coming to use the whole field.

At the other end we did not have the river to provide an open approach. We started right at the end of the field, removing all brush and trees over six feet high. This clearing was a little easier because we did not have to chop the termite hills or remove stumps, and we could let everything lie where it fell. As we worked away from the airstrip, we gradually left the trees a little higher. By the time we were about forty yards away, we only needed to remove the tall trees. We did this to 150 yards out. This made a nice open approach to the field, and pilots would not have to worry about a tree in the way on their approach to landing.

Finally the airstrip was finished. It had been eight months since the message for me came from the sky. I still went out almost daily with one of our guys and kept fussing with this patch or that to make it even smoother. I wanted it to be really good when the first plane arrived. Don had been sending messages at least once a month asking what kind of progress we were making on the airstrip. I had sent a message with the last runner that I was sure we would have it complete by the time the next message arrived. So now I was anxious for the real test. I waited for the five days I knew it would take the runner to get back to Pokwo. Then I started waiting for the airplane. This waiting had a déjà vu feeling to it! Again I kept imagining reasons why the plane had not come. I had a whole list of them, but none of them were true. Ten days after I sent the message found us trying to find ways to keep from real panic. Then a shout came from down the trail, "Hello, Gilo Mission!" I did not know who it was but ran to see. I could hardly believe my eyes. It was Don! I had not thought he would try to walk in due to his health problems and trouble with his legs. I ran to him and gave him a hug that almost knocked us both down.

After we all had a chance to greet him and calm down, Don told us that he wanted to be able to tell the pilot that he personally had inspected the airstrip and that it was ready for use. After Don had something to drink and rested a little, I was anxious to show him the airstrip we had worked so hard on for eight months. I couldn't wait to hear his reaction. It was only a short walk to the edge of the airstrip from camp but you could not actually see it from camp. I walked the short walk with Don, trying to hold down my anxiety and excitement. I thought we had done a good job, considering we had nothing but hand tools. When Don walked out on to the airstrip it was clear that he was amazed. He kept looking around and walking from one side to other. Finally he came over to the four of us together and said, "Boys, I have been living and working in Africa for over twenty years and have seen quite a few airstrips carved out of the bush. This is the first one that was built entirely with hand tools. This airstrip is better than any of those made with machinery!" He then said, "I am amazed! I expected it to be usable but needing a little work. This airstrip is good. It's wider than I asked and it looks to be longer than needed as well." I was both pleased and relieved to have Don confirm that we had indeed done a good job.

Don immediately sent a runner back to Pokwo to have them contact a friend of Don's to make the first flight in. In the meantime, we started work on Don's house. He sent men out to immediately gather more grass for thatch. Even though we were able to save some and gather a little more after the fire, it was not anywhere near enough for Don's house. The trees we saved for building proved to be very useful. In a few days we heard the unmistakable drone of a small plane engine. The pilot flew over the field, Don waved, and the pilot wiggled the wing tips. He made one low pass, turned around, and landed toward us at the camp. There was very little wind so he could have landed either way. He touched down a third of the way down the field and still had to add power to taxi up to where we were waiting. The pilot swung the plane around and shut it off. As soon as he got out he asked, "Is this Gilo International Airport?" We laughed and said, "Yes!" After all, the station, if not the airstrip, had already had one international plane come in from Sudan! The pilot confirmed what Don had said about the airstrip being better than many he had used.

We had a few more flights in the next couple of weeks. Some pilots just wanted to see the new station; most of them brought something in to us. The last one had two pilots. It carried the pilot of the small single-engine airplane that flew in and a commercial pilot who would be flying in the first DC3. Don had said he wanted this airstrip to accommodate DC3s. This was the pilot who would make that first flight. The first flight would carry no passengers and almost no cargo. He had to officially test it with one flight. As soon as the DC3 pilot got out he said what everyone had said, "This is better than many I use. I could have just flown in and landed without this inspection trip." Then the big day arrived. We heard the distinctive rumble of two big rotary engines as the pilot came in fast and low. When he flew over the field, his wheels were not six feet off the ground. When he pulled up at the end, he made an air show turn around by bringing the big plane almost straight up, then making it rotate around the center and come right back down. This time he slowed the plane and landed, touching down close to the end and holding the tail off the ground while taxiing up to us. He was clearly having fun and showing off for us as well. The Gilo River Airstrip was a success. Dr. McClure could get the mission going in earnest.

The first task for the new mission station was to build a house for Don and Lyda. Even though I had seen and participated in building smaller buildings like our dining house, I was not really prepared for the work and materials needed to build a house the size Don was building. It was probably fifty by twenty-five feet wide. So Don sent Anuak workers out looking for posts strong enough and beams long enough for a house of that size. Some of the poles they gathered were long enough and heavy enough to require two or three men to carry them. The framework, outside walls, and roof were completed in about a week.

This was a good thing, because the rains had started. We'd had no rain from the time we arrived until after Don arrived. Clouds began building each day, then one day it rained—and then it rained every day after that, sometimes very heavy rain. So with Don's house secure from the rain, we moved in and used it while more work went on inside. One of the nicest things about being in his house was the lamplight. On one of the airplane trips the pilot brought a can of kerosene and an Aladdin lamp. No, not the kind that produces a genie, although there were many times when one would have been handy. The Aladdin lamp was like the lamp my parents used on our farm before rural electrification. The Aladdin lamp was invented more than one hundred years ago and truly magical in what it is able to do. Ordinary kerosene lamps use a wick. The flame produced by burning the oil is magnified slightly by the glass chimney, but the lamps were always quite smoky. Aladdin lamps are actually incandescent lights like ordinary light bulbs. These lamps use a mantle made of special materials that, when heated, produce a very bright light. An Aladdin lamp produces the equivalent of a 60-watt lightbulb with no smoke. With this wonderful light source our days were much extended. Being able to enjoy a lighted evening in a snug and secure house was quite a treat after the conditions in which we had been living. However, I was beginning to get anxious to return to the States.

CHAPTER TWELVE

GATQWATH, MY BLOOD BROTHER

We had successfully completed the airstrip and were all very proud of our accomplishment. We also were very aware that it was only by the grace of God that we had been able to do what we did. We had been there without a break for eight months, and I was ready for a break. Don asked if I would like to visit a mission station over the border in Sudan where they were working with the Nuer. I jumped at the opportunity. Don had talked about the Nuer from time to time and told us fascinating stories about working in the Sudan. Nuer were close cultural relatives of the Anuak. Nuer and Anuak villages are in both countries and they traditionally live along both sides of the Upper Nile tributaries. The Nuer were a part of the Nilotic tribal groups, along with the Dinka, Anuak, and Shulla. Their languages are all related though distinctly different.

The Nuer tribe raises cattle, as do the Massai in Kenya. All Nilotic people are extremely black in skin color, but the Nuer are taller than the Anuak. Both Anuak and Nuer use a ritual scarification on the forehead of males that signifies a young male becoming a man. The procedure permanently marks one as a member of a particular tribe. The Anuak use rows of bumps on the forehead. The Nuer use rows of long scars on the forehead. The other slightly noticeable difference between Anuak and Nuer is the style of dress. Anuak men always wear some kind of shorts. They may be ragged, torn, and patched, but they are clearly shorts. Sometimes they wear a shirt or jacket they have somehow gotten. Anuak women always wear a skirt and sometimes will wear a Western style dress or smock. Before puberty, boys and girls of either tribe rarely wear any clothes. Young girls nearing puberty usually wear a small apron. Nuer men normally do not wear any clothes. They usually have a string or belt around the waist to carry things. Nuer women wear at least a small apron or skirt.

A couple of short-term (two to three years) missionary women told me of visiting a mission station with the Nuer. They were invited to play a game of volleyball. The women told of their initial embarrassment at not knowing where to look as both men and women jumped for the ball, creating quite a sight for Western eyes! People from Western cultures often think the lack of clothing is at least uncivilized if not immoral, but if you think of the conditions where these people live, it begins to make a lot of sense. It is a very hot climate all year. Clothing picks up, stores, and breeds germs, especially when it cannot be washed often. Clothing is also a wonderful hiding place for insects. If you are not wearing clothes, it is easy to just run down, jump in the river to cool off, wash off, and go right on about your daily life. Wearing no clothing also makes it easy to rub ashes on your body to keep insects away.

Don had arranged for me to meet Chuck at the mission station and put my few things on board the small houseboat that would be my home for the next week. Chuck was going on one of his periodic visits to outlying villages as an agricultural missionary. His primary purpose was to work with the Nuer trying to improve their health through education and demonstration. He also tried to improve their few crops and the health of their animals. That first day we stopped at several villages along the way where Chuck would talk to the people and hand out supplies. At the end of the day we stopped at a larger village and tied up to an actual wooden dock. He said we would be there for several days while he worked with the people in this village and some others within walking distance.

Shortly after we arrived on the first day, a young boy came near and stayed around. Chuck asked his name. He said several words, giving his full name. Then Chuck asked what to call him. He said Gatqwath. Then Chuck told him my name was Dave. I am sure that my attempt at pronouncing his name was at least as strange as when he said, "Dave." He was very kind and patient with me. He would correct me and let me try a word several times; only then would we move on to something else.

The next morning as Chuck left, he told me to just hang around and see what I could learn. Gatqwath showed up

shortly after Chuck left for his trip. I greeted Gatqwath by name
and he greeted me with his version of Dave. By signs and gestures, I got the idea that he would stay around if I wanted him
to. Apparently I succeeded in conveying to him that I would like
that. I started pointing to an object and, with a shrug, indicated
I wanted to know its name. I would do the same with something
I was wearing and then say its name. He got the idea quickly. I
began trying to learn the names of some common things. Eventually, listening to Gatqwath, I picked up a phrase that I thought
meant something like "What is this?" or "What do you call this?"
So I began using that phrase and Gatqwath responded. I might
have wildly misused the phrase. It might have meant something
like, "Stop asking me all these stupid questions. Any fool knows
what that is!" But I employed it to learn the names of a lot of
objects and also plants, birds, cows, goats, etc. When it came
to cows, I quickly learned there were a lot of names, but I was
not able to pick out the subtle (to me) differences. Subsequent
experience strongly suggested that he was being very generous
and kind to me. He clearly wanted to teach me about his life.
After a while we went down near the river. Gatqwath pointed to
or touched everything and then said the name in Nuer. I tried to
remember all of them but failed miserably.

When we got to the river we saw some crocodiles sunning themselves. Gatqwath pointed and proudly said, "Croc!"
He had obviously heard an English speaker call them crocs and
had remembered. He then said the name in Nuer. It may have
been close to what the Anuak called them, but it did not sound

like that to me. Gatqwath then, by gestures, made me understand that they were very dangerous. A croc could take an arm, a leg, or even your life. It was clear he wanted me to understand, I must be very careful that I did not get near them. We then went down where there were dugout canoes tied up. Gatqwath pointed to one and told me its name. Then he picked up the paddle and made rowing motions and told me what that was in Nuer.

The next thing he did really surprised me. He indicated by gestures he would take me in one of the dugouts if I wanted to. I was thrilled at the opportunity even though I could see the crocs watching us. These dugouts are even more unstable than our canoes. Gatqwath was an expert and kept the dugout completely stable while I struggled to get in and not tip us over. I sat down and Gatqwath proceeded to give me a lesson in dugout seamanship. He could maneuver that dugout like our young people maneuver skateboards. I had paddled several different styles of canoes in the States with at least average skill. I thought surely I would be able to handle the dugout. I wanted to show Gatqwath something I was good at. Boy was I wrong! The dugout was extremely difficult to control, even in the very light current with no wind. I managed to get the dugout about twenty feet out and then back to the dock without tipping us over or spinning out of control. Each time I messed up, Gatqwath would use his paddle to keep us under control. It was a very humbling experience. When we got on shore, Gatqwath acted as if I had won a gold medal. He seemed sincerely pleased with my very modest achievement.

I knew just how modest my achievement was. I had seen both Anuak and Nuer men maneuver a heavily loaded dugout on the river in a strong current. They were able to take the dugout from one bank to the other with nothing more than a spear handle the size of my thumb. And they were not using the spear handle to pole the dugout, they used the spear handle like a paddle. We spent the next few days in a similar way, with Gatqwath showing me all he could about his life and the creatures and plants in it. Occasionally we would meet another Nuer. They were always very friendly and pleasant with big smiles. I thoroughly enjoyed myself and it seemed Gatqwath did also.

The morning we were to leave, we packed the boat. After the boat was packed, I told Chuck I wanted to say goodbye to Gatqwath. I wanted to thank him for his help and friendship. I went to find him and met him as he was walking toward the boat. Using gestures, I indicated that we had to leave. Even though hugs were not part of his culture, he allowed me to give him a big hug. He even returned the hug. Then as I was about to leave, he grabbed my arm and tugged on it. He wanted me to go with him, so I did, not knowing what he wanted or where we were going. He led me away from the path we had been on to a cleared area and indicated that he wanted me to kneel down on the ground with him. I did. Then he scooped out a small depression. I didn't know if this was some kind of game or what, but I was willing to go along with it. He had never done anything that was not patient and kind. It was soon clear that this was not a game. When he had finished scooping out the small depression, he helped me lie down on my back with my head over the depression. He put a small piece of pottery under my head in the depression so my head was slightly lifted. The next thing he did still brings tears to my eyes as I remember it. He got his spear, which I knew was very sharp, and brought the head of the spear near my face, and then, making sure I could see him, he laid one finger under the blade of the spear. Then, with his finger between my skin and the blade, drew the spear across my forehead five times. I immediately realized that he was acting out the ritual the Nuer use to bring young boys into full adult membership in the tribe. By ritual, Gatqwath had made me his blood brother! I was overcome with emotion. I felt an overpowering sense of love through this young man. I gave him another big hug with tears streaming down my face. I saw tears in his eyes as well. Although we had only a few spoken words that we could use to communicate, we could and did open our hearts to each other. "Where two or three are gathered, I am there in the middle." God's love was very evident that day.

Since then I have thought often of Gatqwath, his family, and village. When I heard of the terrible atrocities that the Sudanese government inflicted on the people of the southern Sudan, many of whom are Nuer, I felt terrible that all I could do was pray for them. I hope and pray that he and his family are okay.

CHAPTER THIRTEEN

THE RETURN HOME

I would be leaving the Nuer, Gatqwath, and my Anuak friends soon. I had mixed feelings. I was eager to return to the States, to my family and friends, and I was ready and excited about returning to my last year in seminary. On the other hand, I felt real sadness at leaving all this behind, especially since I knew it was unlikely that I would return. As I was leaving, I had no understanding that in less than a year, it would be impossible to return. I certainly would not have planned such an experience as the others and I had; however, it remains one of the most exciting and rewarding experiences of my life. It continues to have a positive impact on my spiritual growth.

The trip back to the United States also had some exciting moments. The DC3 Ethiopian Airline plane that flew me out of Gambela began with one of those moments. The airplane was parked near the small building that served as a terminal. After we were told to board, I entered and chose a seat near the front where I could look out in front of the wing. When we were all boarded—people, chickens, and one goat—they closed the air stair. I was watching for them to bring the external generator to start the engines, but one never came. The pilot tried to start the engines with the airplane's own battery power. The engines were hot from his flight in and would not start. I thought, "Now what? Are we going to have to wait for the engines to cool down, and if we do, does he have enough remaining battery to get them started?" Next thing I knew, I saw a Jeep pulling to the front of the wing near the engine on my side. A man got a stepladder and placed it near the big propeller. Another man handed him a rope about two inches thick, and the man on the ladder began to wrap the rope around the pointed cover (spinner) at the base of the propeller. At first I had no idea what he was doing, but soon I saw him drop the loose end of the rope to the man on the ground who then walked toward the Jeep. Now I knew, but could not believe what I was seeing! He was going to "pull start" this huge engine with the Jeep. When I was a mechanic in the army air unit, I had to prop start quite a few small single-engine airplanes. Even those small engines were often not easy to start. I had never heard of anyone trying what they appeared to be doing.

Shortly, the rope was securely tied to the Jeep's hitch and the driver took up the slack. The man on the ground was standing clear, but in a position so he could see both the pilot and the driver of the Jeep. I saw him signal the Jeep to go. The Jeep started spinning its tires on the gravel. The prop started turning and, all of a sudden, the engine coughed, belched smoke, and started with a roar. It was obvious this was not the first time they had done this; in fact, it looked like this was standard procedure. Once more I saw proof of the adage, "When you do not have what you need, make do with what you have." The Ethiopians continued to amaze me with their ingenuity.

The plane landed for a stop at Gore, where we all got out for awhile. Gore is one of the principal coffee growing regions in Ethiopia. As soon as I got off the plane, I could smell the rich aroma of roasting coffee, good coffee. I did not know until I went to Ethiopia that the coffee bean tree originated in Ethiopia. The legend is that 1,000 years ago a goatherd in the southwestern highlands (exactly where I was) picked some of the red berries from a wild bush and chewed them. He liked the taste and the "feel-good" effect. Whether the legend is true or not, it is true that the Arabica coffee bush still grows wild in these highlands. It is believed that about 600 years ago coffee was taken to Yemen and from there to Saudi Arabia. From there it was introduced to the rest of the world. Ethiopians prepare their coffee similar to espresso, very rich, but not bitter. I can drink Ethiopian coffee without sugar but not espresso. After getting my coffee fix (it didn't take much as I had not had coffee for eight months), we again boarded the plane. This time they had an external generator to start the airplane.

I flew out of Addis on Ethiopian Airlines. To my surprise and great pleasure the pilot was Lem Tew, a TWA pilot working for the Ethiopian Airlines. I had met Lem earlier by way of Dr. McClure. He greeted me warmly and quietly told me after we got airborne to come up to the cabin. We were leaving Addis just after sundown on a beautiful clear night. When the announcement came that we could remove our seatbelts, I got up and went to the cabin. The cabin door was open so I tapped on Lem's shoulder. When he saw me, he folded down the jump seat between the two pilots' seats and said, "Have a seat." I was shocked and very pleased. Lem knew that I had been a helicopter mechanic in the army and I really liked flying. I asked, "Is this all right?" He said, "Sure, up here I say what can be done. You can ride up here and see our initial descent into Cairo, and with any luck you'll get a great view of the pyramids. When we begin our final descent I'll have you move back to your seat." I had a wonderful time visiting with him and watching the flight procedures. As far as I could tell, we were the only airplane in that part of the sky. It was a gorgeous, full moon night, and the pyramids stood out clearly as we descended into the airport.

From Cairo I flew to Rome and spent a day there, overwhelmed once more with all the historical sites. I then flew to Amsterdam where, by the gracious help of Dr. McClure, I would pick up a new bright red VW Beetle. Don had arranged for me to stay at a boardinghouse he knew, and be taken to pick up the car. I took a taxi from the airport to the boardinghouse. When I got there, the man and his wife greeted me warmly as a friend of their "wonderful friend Dr. McClure." They showed me my room where I left my duffel bag. They then invited me to have the evening meal with them. I thanked them, but told them I was not feeling well, and preferred not to eat. They then became very solicitous and insisted that they take me to the pharmacist. I tried to tell them it was not necessary, especially since it was after the pharmacy had closed. They still insisted and told me it would be no bother, the pharmacist was a friend of theirs and lived over the pharmacy just a few houses away. They took me to him, and he was as gracious as they were and insisted on getting me some medicine for my stomach. (I guess I had something in Rome that did not agree with me.) When I asked how much it was so I could pay him, he refused any money and insisted I take it with no charge.

With the help of my new friends, I picked up my new VW the next day. I drove from the Netherlands through Germany and into Austria where I stayed overnight. I was traveling on a very tight budget, so for the four days I traveled in Europe I ate bread and cheese, a few pastries, and drank wine or beer. While driving through Bavaria, I stopped at a German beer house and ordered a beer. The woman brought me my beer in a stein that I am sure held more than a quart of beer. The look on my face must have made her think there was something wrong with the beer. There was nothing wrong with the beer, it was just four times more than I could drink. Not only could I not drink that much, I wouldn't have if I could. I was still driving. I drank only about a third of it, if that, and left the rest with a big tip.

I drove to Austria where I stayed in a boardinghouse in Vienna for a couple of days. While there, I took a drive into Switzerland, mostly just to see what it was like. I wasn't much impressed. I liked Austria much better and wished that I could have spent more time there. I drove back to Rotterdam the next day and took advantage of the Autobahn. It really is without speed limit. I was driving 70 mph, and most everyone passed me like I was hardly moving. That certainly helped me get to Rotterdam quickly.

Rotterdam was where I would board the freighter to New York and where they would load my new car onboard. Again it was a Norwegian ship. I was not sorry, as I so enjoyed the first one. Also, having eaten very little the last week, I was starving. I had been able, with Dr. McClure's help, to get a package deal that included a one-night stay in a hotel in Rotterdam. I would drop my car off at the loading dock the night before our departure; they would take me to the hotel and pick me up in the morning. All this, my passage, and the freight for the car were all in one package.

The voyage from Rotterdam to New York was uneventful. I ate, slept, read, and repeated it all. The trip took only five days this time. We arrived at the dock in New York at night, sometime after midnight. Unfortunately, I was sound asleep when we passed Lady Liberty on our return voyage. We would be able to get breakfast onboard and then disembark. I asked the captain if it would be all right if I cleared my cabin and waited until my car was off loaded. He told me I could stand at the rail, below the bridge, that looked over the holds where they would be unloading the freight. I watched while they removed the huge doors that covered the hatches to the hold. Then they began using the onboard crane to pick up loads, lift them out, and place them on the dock or on trucks. While waiting for my car to appear, I was idly listening to the dock workers chatter among themselves. Suddenly I realized that I had been listening without hearing. I had expected not to understand their "foreign" language, so I didn't. I had been used to hearing people speak without understanding them for nearly a year. It's true that their heavy Brooklyn accents did sound strange, and even when I realized it was English I was hearing, I had to work to understand. Finally I saw my little red car come swinging out of the hold on a sling; it swung over the side and was set down on the dock. I was back home and ready to go.

My experience working and traveling with Dr. Don McClure and his wife, Lyda, remains one of the most meaningful and certainly the most life-changing event of my life. It was also the perfect healing I needed to recover from my wife's sudden death during my first year in seminary. Upon my return to the States, I completed my study at Pittsburgh Theological Seminary. While completing the last year of seminary, I had the opportunity to share my Ethiopia experience with hundreds of churches and other groups. That, too, was very enjoyable. Sharing with others allowed me to relive that year many times.

To the readers of this book, I thank you for joining me once more on this adventure. I hope you also received joy and, perhaps, some inspiration from the reading.

May you continue to be blessed on your personal adventure wherever it takes you.

APPENDIX

INTRODUCTION TO ETHIOPIA 1961

Almost everything we did in 1961 would not have been possible two or three years later. In 1961 Ethiopia and Eritrea were linked in an ill-fated federation conceived by Western Allies after World War II. Haile Selassie, the emperor of Ethiopia at that time, was generally considered to be a relatively benevolent emperor. It was, in fact, due to his friendship that Dr. Don McClure was allowed to do the work he accomplished. Haile Selassie was heir to a dynasty that traced its lineage, at least by tradition, back to King Solomon and the Queen of Sheba.[1] Haile Selassie was not able to tolerate the Eritreans' desire for full independence. In 1962 he unilaterally annexed Eritrea and brought it under his authoritarian rule, only one year after our trip. After Haile Selassie took this action, we may not have been allowed to travel between the two countries as we did.

---

1. "Haile Selassie I," Biography.com, http://www.biography.com/people/haile-selassie-i-9325096 (accessed Jun 15, 2012).

Eritrea is one of the oldest countries in the world. It was known as Punt, meaning God's Land, by the ancient Egyptians. It was first mentioned in Egyptian writings dating to 25 BC. The country takes its name, Eritrea, meaning red, from the name of the Red Sea, which was then known as the Sea of Eritrea. The Italians colonized Eritrea toward the end of the nineteenth century, bringing many European-style improvements in areas of education, medicine, and agriculture. They also made major improvements in the infrastructure: paved roads, electrical power, the railroad, and the Asmara-Massawa Cableway.

Before the dictator Mussolini rose to power in 1922, the Italian administration employed many Eritreans to fill positions in police departments, public works, and other public service areas. After Mussolini rose to power, his megalomania caused the removal of all Eritreans from such positions of service. The British captured Eritrea in 1941 and administered the country until 1950 when the United States, Britain, and others decided, in spite of the clear desire of Eritreans to be independent, to link Ethiopia and Eritrea in a loose federation. Eritrea's culture and history as a democratic state were alien to Ethiopia's history as an imperial state, then ruled by the Emperor Haile Selassie.

Amharic is the official language of Ethiopia. The Amhara tribe has been the ruling tribe for many centuries. This long period of ruling dominance ended with the death of Haile Selassie in 1974. Ethiopia takes pride in being a very diverse country. There are at least seventy-seven different ethnic groups or tribes, each with its own distinct language. The three largest groups are the Oromo, Amhara, and Tigreans. These three to-gether make up more than two thirds of the country's approxi-mately 84 million people.

In the 1970s, Ethiopia experienced severe famine. This was at the same time Soviet-led Marxists were instigating rebel-lion. A faction of the Ethiopian military deposed Haile Selassie on September 12, 1974. He was imprisoned and later died in prison. While officially denied, it is believed that he was assassi-nated while in prison because of his esteem among the common people of Ethiopia. In 1991 after the fall of Mengistu, the So-viet-supported dictator of Ethiopia, Eritrea once more achieved independence, although it has been a continuing struggle to maintain its independence.

I have described how people lived and their culture as I experienced it in 1961. Much has changed since that time. Many of the Anuak and Nuer have adopted Western ways and no longer live in the old traditional way; however, there are still many thousands who do continue to live in the old way. Due to the political upheavals and severe drought, their lives are truly desperate.

The Gilo River is very near the border of Ethiopia and Sudan. In fact in places, the river is the border. Dr. Don McClure had permission to start the work that we were a part of. How-ever, it became more and more difficult for Don to continue the work due to the growing and escalating conflict between Sudan and Ethiopia. That border area became a war zone. Don tried to move his work to tribes in southern Ethiopia near Somalia.

Somalia is a harpoon-shaped strip of very arid land enclosing the entire tip of the Horn of Africa and a strip along Ethiopia's southeastern border. This land has been the home of nomadic Muslim tribes since the seventh century. While the land is very arid, its seaports are highly valued. The border between Ethiopia and Somalia has been in dispute for centuries. The present arbitrary border was established in 1960 when Britain and Italy granted independence to lands they had ruled as colonies since the 1920s. Ethiopia seized the Ogeden Desert early in the colonial period, claiming it as historical Ethiopian lands. However, that region was still the land of Muslim nomadic tribes who had little or no regard for borders. In 1977 the military rulers of Somalia openly backed guerillas that were rebelling against the Ethiopian government.

In March 1977, Don McClure was murdered by those same outlaw guerillas, funded and supplied with weapons and ammunition by the Soviet Union. The purpose seemed to be only to foment unrest, create chaos, and foster terror among people who only wanted to live in peace and not be bothered by any government. A full account of his life and work has been written by Charles Partee.[2]

The internal war between North Sudan and South Sudan has roots that go back prior to British rule. The northern, mostly Arabic and Muslim people have entrenched hostility toward the "black" primitives of the south. The current human

---

2. Charles Partee, *Adventure in Africa: The Story of Don McClure*, University Press of America, 2000.

disaster is only this epoch's manifestation of deep-seated racial and cultural prejudice. "The Lost Boys of Sudan"[3] are only a piece of that tragedy.

Our volunteer group was directly impacted by early hints of the border conflict. The airplane that flew us into the Gilo River site was based in Sudan by Missionary Aviation Fellowship (MAF). It was allowed to make flights one day and not allowed after that. I was able to travel into the southern Sudan to visit missionaries working with the Nuer tribe. I would not have been allowed to do that perhaps even a year later. The Nuer, Dinka, and Anuak tribes, also known collectively as Nilotics, are all culturally and linguistically related. Their traditional homelands reach across several borders of present-day countries Sudan, Ethiopia, Eritrea, and Kenya. These artificial borders present many difficulties for people who've never known national boundaries.

The northern ruling body of Sudan actively promoted or, at the very least, allowed systematic attacks including enslavement of the southern people. They allowed thousands to starve and prevented aid from reaching them.

A referendum took place in southern Sudan January 9–15, 2011, to vote on the question of independence of South Sudan from North Sudan. The results were reported as 98.8 percent voting in favor of independence. Even allowing for voting irregularities, the vote was overwhelmingly in favor of independence. On July 9, the government of South Sudan declared

3.   http://www.lostboysfilm.com/about.html

its independence from the rest of Sudan and named Juba the capital of South Sudan, the world's newest state. The hope is that the situation for tribes in South Sudan will improve greatly.

In Ethiopia it has not been a great deal better than in Sudan. There is still a deeply ingrained prejudice in the highland people, who are of the same genetic origin as Indian and Near Eastern people, against the lowland "black" people who are of Nilotic origin or, as we used to say, "Negroid." Currently in Ethiopia this prejudice is being exploited to justify brutality, massacres, and ultimately the confiscation of rich agricultural land on the Upper Nile watershed. These lands historically belong mostly to the Anuak tribe. So it is convenient for the government to use deep-rooted prejudice to take over these lands and exploit them for the wealth of a few.

The Ethiopia of 2012 is not the Ethiopia of 1961. My fellow volunteers and I were extremely fortunate to have been there at that time. We were there when this adventure was possible. It is not today.

The Geology of Ethiopia

When I pulled up a map of part of Africa showing Ethiopia and the Arabian Peninsula, I was reminded of a story I heard some time ago about a teacher telling her grade school class about world geography. She had the children gather around a large globe and started talking about different places. One young girl held up her hand. The teacher, a little impatient as she had not finished her story, finally told the girl to go ahead. The little girl said, "Teacher, it looks like South America and Africa could fit together. Were they once hooked together?" The teacher said, "That's ridiculous! They were never together; they have always been this way." Out of the mouth of babes…

If you look at a topographical map showing the Arabian Peninsula and Ethiopia, you can see where they did fit together. The tip of the peninsula, which is Yemen, fits nicely in the slot over Djibouti and into the heart of Ethiopia. The Arabian plate and the African plate are sliding apart, normally at about the same rate as fingernails grow. But in 2005, the rift changed dramatically. In a few weeks, the rift grew as much as eight meters as the two plates were forced apart. This process is the key to understanding the topography of Ethiopia. The rift valley begins in the Dead Sea and goes through the Red Sea, turns a corner at Djibouti, and cuts through Ethiopia and on down into Kenya. If you look at a topographical map of Ethiopia you can clearly see this valley and the string of lakes that follow it. This extremely rugged piece of real estate, which is now Ethiopia, appeared around 75 million years ago when the Earth's crust uplifted a large dome of rock. The fracturing over millions of years produced much volcanic activity that helped build this uniquely rugged, mountainous country. Most of the country is above 5,000 feet and has peaks up to 15,000 feet. There is no other area in Africa like this.

On a topographic map of Ethiopia, you can see how rugged this county is. Gambela is in the little point of Ethiopia pointing west. Addis Ababa, the capital, is nearly in the center, not far from the rift valley, up in the highlands. On the northern border of Ethiopia where it connects to Eritrea is the rugged escarpment where Eritrea borders the Red Sea. Ethiopia is landlocked. That is one reason they have tried to claim the lands of Eritrea.

Dr. McClure and we four boys drove from Massawa, Eritrea to Gambela beginning at the Dead Sea. We climbed the escarpment pushed up by the rift, drove through the pushed up highland region, and went down the western edge of that tectonic upheaval to the Nile plain.

ABOUT THE AUTHOR

David E. Breckenridge, MDiv, MS, MSW, is a retired Presbyterian minister, missionary and a retired clinical social worker. He continues to manage their Flint Hills native grass ranch in Kansas. He is the devoted and admiring husband of his wife Marcia. They have three grandchildren and three children. Due to varied job experiences they have lived in several states with their two little dogs, Woolie and Auggie. They are currently thinking about another move. The author is an enthusiastic supporter of renewable resources and a sustainable future for all the world's grandchildren.

The author is deeply interested in exploring ways to help build bridges between Christians holding to the "Old time religion" and those Christians wishing to explore different expressions of their Christian faith. He believes the imagery of language may be the key to opening our hearts and minds to each other.

For more about the author, his continued spiritual journey and possible future books;

Check out the author's website at:

DavidBreckenridgeAuthor.com